Key Words

Key Words

Reclaiming Children's Precious Vocabulary

Cory Gann

ROWMAN & LITTLEFIELD
Lanham • Boulder • New York • London

Published by Rowman & Littlefield
A wholly owned subsidiary of The Rowman & Littlefield Publishing Group, Inc.
4501 Forbes Boulevard, Suite 200, Lanham, Maryland 20706
www.rowman.com

Unit A, Whitacre Mews, 26–34 Stannary Street, London SE11 4AB

Copyright © 2018 by Cory Gann

All rights reserved. No part of this book may be reproduced in any form or by any electronic or mechanical means, including information storage and retrieval systems, without written permission from the publisher, except by a reviewer who may quote passages in a review.

British Library Cataloguing in Publication Information Available

Library of Congress Cataloging-in-Publication Data

ISBN: 978-1-4758-3827-5 (cloth) ISBN: 978-1-4758-3828-2 (pbk.) ISBN: 978-1-4758-3829-9 (electronic)

To my daughters, Megan and Caitlin, who hold the keys to my heart.
To the memory of Renie, their mom and my first love.
To Cher, who taught me that love only grows
like a candle lighting more candles.
And . . . to the memory of Matthew Schwartz
who gave me the honor of being his kindergarten teacher.

Contents

Foreword		ix
Preface		xi
Acknowledgments		xv
Opening Quotations		xvii
1	Unlocking the Key Word Approach	1
2	Roots and History	9
3	The System	25
4	Key Words: A Natural Fit	43
5	Cultural Excavation	71
6	Movements: Bounding into Writing	89
7	The Whimsy of Key Words	107
8	Books: Authored and Produced in the Classroom	131
Bibliography		141
About the Author		145

Foreword

It may be surprising to some of your readers that I am writing this foreword to *Key Words: Reclaiming Children's Precious Vocabulary*, since the focus of my work is antibias education. However, the pedagogy of "key words," first developed by Sylvia Ashton-Warner (1963), *is* a part of the larger arena of equity in education. In fact, finding the work of Ashton-Warner had a profound effect on me in my own formative years as an educator. Her book *Teacher* was a revelation. It opened my eyes to how important teaching methods beyond traditional western European and American approaches are for fully fostering the development of *all* children. It also reinforced my understanding that reading and writing literacy are vital for children to prosper in diverse societies, as well as fundamental tools for creating social change for justice for all.

Therefore, I was delighted when Cory Gann, a once-upon-a time Pacific Oaks College colleague and a member of the original ABC Task Force (*Anti-Bias Curriculum: Tools for Empowering Young Children*), showed me the manuscript of this book. It was exciting to read, taking me back to my early discovery of the "key word" literacy development approach *and* forward to a relevant approach to literacy development for today's children. Cory has impressively integrated his own understanding of antibias, culturally sensitive education with teaching children to read and write.

The writing is clear and very accessible. The wonderful stories beautifully illuminate how young children engage in literacy learning and how teachers engage with the children. *Key Words: Reclaiming Children's Precious Vocabulary* is also a book that will be informative and useful for everyone. If you are learning to be an early childhood teacher or a new practicing teacher, you will learn about an exciting approach to children's literacy development. If you are an experienced teacher, you will expand your repertoire. Happy reading and teaching.

—Louise Derman-Sparks, Pasadena, California
Anti-Bias Education for Young Children &
Ourselves Leading Anti-Bias Early Childhood
Programs: A Guide for Change

Preface

There is a question that has nagged at me for a lot of years.

When I first trained as an early childhood education teacher, I learned about key words. Then, I became a kindergarten teacher and made sure to include a key word approach as part of the reading program. Years later, I became a teacher educator and have had the opportunity to observe in hundreds of early childhood classrooms. A question started to nag at me.

Maybe it has been a slow wondering ache for as long as I have been an early childhood educator. Why is it rare to see key words inside of classrooms where young children are learning to read?

To be sure, there are laudable programs, in preschools and kindergartens and first grades where children get to use important words that are special. And there is lots of good writing instruction going on in lots of classrooms. Teachers experiment with all kinds of techniques in order to scaffold their students over the literacy hump and into a realm where they feel that they can *do* reading and writing.

A kindergarten teacher I observed was well known in the school for teaching his charges to scribble—an approach based on the developmental theory that scribbling is a stage the child traverses on the way to genuine letter and word formation. It gets them started as journal keepers, and this class's day started with everyone scribbling away in their notebooks. Eventually, real letters appear.

Why couldn't key words be a component of what transpired in that classroom?

I have seen lots of guided writing instruction as a manner of laying the ground work for students to become writers. Really appealing mini-lessons happen where the teacher models writing about something that happened to her over the weekend. Or what her favorite pet is. Kindergartners sit dutifully on the carpet and offer suggestions for what the next sentence might be. And the teacher jots down a list of words that are important so that there is an instant word bank for these novice writers to refer to once they are dismissed to their own desks and their own journals to "write" about a similar topic.

Why are key words not at hand?

A most common literacy system is one in which the children simply get out their journals at writing time. Each day there is a new entry. For many, it is a matter of drawing a picture. Then later in the year, words get added to the picture. Perhaps, there is a prompt of some kind: My favorite food is . . . In many classrooms I've visited (I'm confident to say hundreds) I've wondered how come a key word dimension is not part of these literacy regimens. I have theory. And it goes a good way in explaining why I set upon writing the book that follows. More about that later.

I have also watched and facilitated children doing key words. Among several general appraisals I could render, there is the most important one: doing key words is highly motivating. There is a self-generating drive to do them. It cuts across skill level. Children for whom the alphabet is still fuzzy and elusive and children who have already got sound-symbol relationships down are motivated to work at key words. In chapter 6, I quote *doing words* guru Katie Johnson about how easy it was to start a key program. She said it was almost like she wasn't working. Children take to it naturally.

There are a lot of reasons a teaching initiative can be easy or hard, but ultimately it has to do with motivation. With key words, the teacher doesn't have to say "this is going to be so fun" or "this is easy." It just starts and it's a magnet that pulls students in. Teachers don't have to say "you've earned extra recess" or "the class gets five points because people were on task." Key words have a way of keeping people on task.

Why is it hard to find key word programs inside of classrooms?

In this book, you will be introduced to or become reacquainted with Sylvia Ashton-Warner, who is renowned for bringing key words (or the key vocabulary as she named it) into the public eye. Her book about using key words, *Teacher*, caught the reading public by storm and popularized this literacy approach even among consumers not engrossed in schooling matters. The headline of the *New York Times* book review in 1963 read, "It's not the what; it's the how." An important component of key word theory is that the process is very important. Chapter 3 talks a lot about the process.

I have seen key words done in some classrooms. For the most part, these are initiatives undertaken in progressive child-centered environments—schools that tend to live in and serve prosperous communities and families that have a track record of generations of success in school. The demographics of such programs are white, middle- or upper-middle-class, dominant culture. That is an irony given that Sylvia Ashton-Warner's career was predominantly teaching Maori children in New Zealand—an indigenous population that has suffered conquest, colonization, and marginalization akin to other indigenous nations.

This book is written in and from the belief system that in the United States, black and brown children, children who live in poverty, children about whom the term *opportunity gap* was coined, not only deserve but must also demand the most innovative, motivating, and higher-order thinking approaches to literacy development that can be designed or reclaimed. And *reclaimed* is really what it is about. Children *have* the words that are key for them. New key words crop up all the time. Laying claim to them inside their own classrooms—that is what this book is about.

Back to my theory. Every child has a set of key words that is different from every other child in the class. There is a story behind each word. Teaching with a key word approach forces the teacher away from standardization and smack dab toward differentiation. It is a differentiation of the how and the what—process and content. It is daunting to tackle something that is so individualized, and my theory speculates that being so differentiated is just the barrier that keeps a key word approach from showing up in many classrooms.

However, should any teacher react by saying "good idea but it doesn't work with a class of twenty-five or thirty," a good reminder is that some teachers have found that they have never had an easier time getting a literacy program started than when they introduced the process of key words. Children working on key words are immersed in literacy. When it comes to running an early childhood classroom, that kind of engagement is key.

Author's Note:

The following pages contain many stories from different early childhood classrooms. Almost all of the stories were observed first hand. Occasionally, details were obtained via interview. Names of children and teachers have been changed.

Acknowledgments

Leah Tangen had helped a neighbor with editing of a documentary and like magic she jumped all in to the rigorous process of helping prepare this manuscript. It was remarkable the way we were on the same page editing away at our own desktops, and then meeting for coffee.

Louise Derman-Sparks—if you are an ECE person, you know she is an icon. Counting Louise as a professional colleague and a friend is a true honor.

Danny Peary and Jeanie Dooha have been my inspirations for tackling and staying with this project. They embody the creative vent and they have modeled the maxim to write and do art about what you know and love.

Joanne Bowers, Nancy Place, and Barb Padden read early versions of the manuscript and provided invaluable feedback.

My Praxis colleagues are the people who inspire me and keep my mind fresh: Cynthia VanLoo, Charlotte Jahn, Fran Davidson, Nnenna Odim, and Dominique Alex. And, of course, our president emeritus, Debra Sullivan. The perspective I have about equity literacy I owe to them.

I am indebted to my colleagues at Central Washington University who practice "lived experience" scholarship every day: Don Woodcock, Melanie Kingham, Yukari Amos, and the very devoted members of the Diversity and Equity Committee: Bobby Cummings, Kathleen Barlow, Charles Lix, Susanna Flores, Kandee Cleary and Mateo Artuega.

My early childhood education roots are grounded at Los Angeles Family School and Pacific Oaks Children's School. Vicki Rank and Mae Varon were my teachers about nurturing young children. Liz Deardorff was my first teaching fellow and taught me as much as I taught her.

Above all, I send appreciation to Cher who practiced amazing patience throughout the preparation of this manuscript and provided important feedback for earlier drafts.

As a teacher, professor, and practicum student supervisor I have had the honor to watch so many children develop and blossom and to observe hundreds of teachers grow as brilliant educators. Here is an acknowledgment and appreciation to every one of them.

Opening Quotations

First words must be already a part of the dynamic life. First books must be made of the stuff of the child herself, whatever and wherever the child.

—Sylvia Ashton-Warner

Every day is a new collection of images to share, a new delineation of the class as the answers to "What is your word today?" pile up in the basket. One year, the first day of Doing Words in kindergarten, these were read in the circle: Mommy. Duchess. baby. Wayne. Mommy. Easter. horse. Smiley. Horace. Snoopy. fire. Gloria. Grampy. Mommy. Francis. Darren. Dad. fire. Tiny. zebra. Mom. birthday. Wonder Woman. Chieftan. rocket. Mama.

—Katie Johnson

"They're not thinking about what they're writing about or what I'm teaching. I'm teaching about 'bed' and 'can' but they were thinking about canoes and grandfathers and drowned men and eels. It seems to me . . . I seem so rude to intrude."

Keith responds, "That's just it. Well dear, that's what we're paid to do, just that: intrude."

—Sylvia Ashton-Warner

She would come to understand that a child who is full of news, confusion, wonder must express it before he or she can attend to the teacher's lesson.

—Sydney Clemens

She had encountered children's resistance to the prescribed curriculum and came to believe that canned, colonial curriculum did intellectual harm.

—Sydney Clemens

The primary word is not a straightforward symbol for a concept but rather an image, a picture, a mental sketch of a concept, a short tale about it—indeed a small work of art.

—Lev Vygotsky

The Maori children Sylvia taught were caught squarely between two cultures, two languages, two value systems. What finally made Sylvia's work with the children effective was the artist in her communicating with the artist in them.

—Sydney Clemens

While her reputation is based on her method of teaching young children to read . . . Sylvia often declared that all of her work was in the service of peace.

—Sydney Clemens

Katie Johnson's "Doing Words" Program: Six Movements (Stages)
"I like to think of these stages as Movements. There is something satisfyingly symphonic about the way organic writing works with children."

—Katie Johnson

The illustrations that are seen by the inner eye are organic, and it is the captioning of these that I call the "key vocabulary."

—Sylvia Ashton-Warner

Just as the toddler bursts into speech because representing words is powerful and interesting, young children who study key vocabulary burst into reading, craving the written symbol for its power and magic.

—Sydney Clemens

Chapter 1

Unlocking the Key Word Approach

Lists are everywhere in classrooms that serve children in their early learning years. There are list of rules, list of class members, list of lunch items, homework records, emergency procedures, favorite authors, math strategies, and geometric shapes. And there are, of course, many lists related to reading and writing. The following are two lists of words. They have decidedly different sources.

    here   sister
    come   Richie
    see   birthday party
    what   gracias

It's not a matter of one list being good and one being bad. These are all great words. The words in the left-hand column derive from the Dolch Compendium of the first 100 sight words to be learned. The words in the right-hand column are from the key word rings of kindergarten and first graders who have generated their own words while working in a program called organic reading.

These lists work together and they are both important. One cannot function without the other. To learn how to read and write, children need to know about and be comfortable with the most frequently used words of everyday speech. They also need to see and create the words that have special meaning in their own unique and magical worlds. That is their *key vocabulary*.

There are many systems and curricula for inculcating the 100 most common words. It happens in every classroom. Less often do children participate in a systematic program for developing their own key words. This is a book about getting at, hearing, knowing, writing down, and learning the key words of young children. It is also about taking those words and giving them flight into the stratosphere of writing and wordsmithing. This is a book about literacy.

BREAKING THROUGH WITH A JACKHAMMER

The inspiration for key words was kindled by a teacher and writer named Sylvia Ashton-Warner who taught four-, five-, and six-year-old children in the decades spanning the 1940s to early 1970s. Teachers in training learn about Sylvia Ashton-Warner as part of historical context and introduction to early childhood education. She is one of the luminary pioneers and iconic figures alongside the likes of Maria Montessori, Janice Hale, Lev Vygostsky, and Jean Piaget, who share the responsibility and accolade of elevating early childhood education (ECE) into the ranks of educational specialization. Ashton-Warner's *Teacher* is the best-selling classic, and *Spinster* actually made its way onto the silver screen starring Shirley McClaine.

While these are the most famous of her books and launch the key word story, other Ashton-Warner titles go deeper into her autobiographical process. The actual autobiography is entitled *I Passed This Way*, and together with *Spearpoint* it fully flushes out the philosophy that this teacher-writer used to meld her life, her teaching, her creative drive, and her revelatory insight about the inner worlds of children into an approach having to do with the advent of the skills of reading and writing.

Chapter 2 is devoted to an extensive discussion of Ashton-Warner's ideas and theory—the postulation of a literacy method built around the distinctive, special, and differentiated words that have significant meaning for the individual child. Discover a child's special words, give them back to her on durable card stock, and watch her read them as solidly embedded pictographs of the referents they bear—that was it in a nutshell. Each child possesses her or his key vocabulary. The pedagogical question was how to structure a curriculum that allows this dynamic interchange to happen in a class of twenty or twenty-five children in an active kindergarten or first-grade classroom.[1]

Every kindergarten class begins with a few get-to-know-each-other weeks in which routines are taught and these young children are encouraged to share something of their lives. Attentive teachers observe and watch for the unique backgrounds and stories that make each student an individual personality in the group. For example, in her year-long chronicle about teaching literacy in a kindergarten classroom, *Look, I Made a Book*, Nina Zaragoza explains that her group time structure with the acronym TAG called for her five-year-olds to *tell* what they like, *ask* questions, and *give* suggestions.[2]

Teacher barometers are exceedingly informative about the appropriate time to kick in structured and formal learning programs especially in language arts where TAG activities blend into early lessons of writing and reading. In Zaragoza's class, they got started right away with blank books, pencils, and crayons at the ready beckoning novice writers to jumpstart their authorship careers.

Regie Routman revealed in her treatise about teaching reading, *Reading Essentials*,[3] that she was always primed on day one to field student hesitancy about learning to read. When a September chorus of "But I can't read" contagiously reverberated around the room, she got the ball rolling by saying "I guarantee you will be able to read by the time the week is over." Then, she would announce, "We're going to write a book together right now." A "We Can" big book was immediately in the works written in tandem by teacher and children.

Doing key words (Katie Johnson used the term *doing words* in her book by the same title) follows the same self-fulfilling spirit that puts children into the role of readers in a way that is supportive of and complementary to adopted reading curriculum and instruction. The teacher is saying, "I just know that if I give you a card with a word on it that is special to you, you will own that word and will know what the card says."

A key words program usually starts with a call to parents requesting that each student bring in a shoebox, which will become the home and grand central station for key word enterprises. Into these boxes is placed a selection of card stock cards, some pencils, and crayons. There is also a key ring—so very important.

Teachers discover or rediscover one of those truisms about grand projects in early childhood: you start by starting. Every teacher's first foray into organic reading is an exploration and process of discovery—how all this will work with the particular group of children who have shown up this year. Katie Johnson talks about "new decisions every year," which nicely captures the fluidity of a teacher's life. There is no prefab teacher's kit with tabulated cards and spiral-bound grade-level instruction manuals. There is the shoe box of material and a not-yet-excavated gold mine of key vocabulary. But the vigor and enthusiasm that children bring to the process help provide structure and a feedback loop of motivation to keep all of it going. Here's what happened in one classroom:

Matthew arrived at school, bursting with pride and story. He was a poster child of TAG, especially the tell part because he had spent the weekend as his dad's sidekick, who had rented a jackhammer in order to loosen and replace a large section of concrete in front of their house. Matthew was abuzz with descriptions about the whir of the machine and the vibrating father that its use had produced.

"Have you ever done a jackhammer?" was Matthew's inquiry to his teacher.

"Nope, I sure haven't." she replied, followed with a question back to him, "Have you ever had jackhammer as a key word?"

"What?" he giggled, "Jackhammer's not a key word!"

"Maybe not, but don't tell that to the jackhammer."

Later that day, Matthew was tracing *jackhammer* on a piece of key word card stock after insisting that jackhammer would be his first key word for the day. He collected other words during the afternoon, but jackhammer was the one he kept coming back to, sharing with others, studying, and reading. Toward the end of the day, the key word group had become quite independent, sharing words, elaborating on illustrations, and telling the stories sparked by the word captions. At the corner of the table, there was an amusing sight: Matthew was jackhammering the air in front of him, both hands gripped on the "handle" of the card stock card that he had scissor-chiseled into the shape of a jackhammer. Having appropriately vibrated along with the machine, he said out loud to no one in particular, "Time to put the ol' jackhammer back in its key word box."

Teaching reading, and writing can be serious business. But the joy of literacy must not be forgotten or neglected. It is a leitmotif throughout all of schooling, whether named as such or not. There is a whimsy about it that cannot be denied. Stories of such whimsy, such as Matthew's, are sprinkled throughout the following pages. They are intertwined with history and theory in order to provoke joyful reflection.

A MAGICAL PROCESS

Matthew and countless other children have in their own right been teachers about their captivating process of *doing words*. This is a dynamic that has been well chronicled and theorized about, but it is one thing to understand the concept of key words and quite another to be immersed in these interactions and to discover the learning that takes place.

Every transaction is a story with a route travelled by the student in which a key word is identified, discovered, and written, and then may inspire a continuation of the tale. This word may be overheard by other classmates, it may lead to a long discussion, and it may become the focus of elaboration and the prompt for a longer expostulation. These mutations and developments are the stuff of fluid composition, which is why Katie Johnson expanded upon the system and detailed a progression of *Movements* through which young children become writers. They are learning to write the word and their world.

CONSISTENT WITH EMERGENT LITERACY

A key word approach is consistent with the best and most distinguished of early childhood literacy theory. The hallmark of teaching and learning during pre-K and kindergarten matriculation is emergent literacy—a view of becoming literate that pays attention to predictable developmental stages a child will traverse. For example, most children learn to write alphabet letters randomly as part of their pretend play at writing, until sound-symbol connections eventually lead these same learners to choose letters consistently, based on phonetic tags.

C is used when a four-year-old wants to spell *CAT*. In pedagogical parlance, this use of *inventive spelling* follows along a continuum of writing development. Just as a child's name is one of his or her first *sight words*, the drive to gain a core of such key words is very much in keeping with the developmental process. As students graduate into first and later grades, they will extend their writing into sentences, stories, and extensive narratives.

Teachers are well versed in the fact that children's own experiences are the stories that bootstrap their narratives into more and more sophisticated terrain. Such ideas form the basis of writing theory offered by Lucy Calkins, Donald Graves, and other respected educators who have promoted children capturing *small moments* as the content of their prose. These methodologies put the writer and her experiences front and center, casting the teacher as an excavator and helping the young student discover the writing within her.

KEY WORDS AND ALIGNMENT WITH PROFESSIONAL STANDARDS

A key word program is in line with standards and supports the intent and language of the standards that are nationally set in order to advance language arts across the curriculum. Additionally, state, school district, and professional standards all serve as backdrops for emergent literacy implementation, of which key words can be an instrumental component. The compatibility between these criteria and key words is most appreciated by listing some of the seminal professional and common core standards that are mainstays in program review.

The following is taken from the National Association for the Education of Young Children (NAEYC) Professional Standards for Literacy:

- The main components of literacy—listening, speaking, reading, and writing—should all be encouraged through participation with adults and peers in conversations and activities that are meaningful to the child. Each

child's interest and motivation to engage in literacy-related activities are evident before that child is able to read or write conventionally.
- Children develop their ability to converse at length and in depth on a topic in various settings (e.g., one-on-one with adults and peers, in small groups).
- Children associate reading and writing with pleasure and enjoyment as well as with skill development.

Conversation and motivation are fundamental values in programs that utilize key word activities.

Key words are inherently aligned with Common Core Standards. In fact, these standards fortify the assertion that key word work is founded upon the most widely accepted best practices of literacy education. Students in the early years of schooling are expected to acquire foundational skills with regard to print concepts, phonological awareness, phonics and word recognition, and comprehension and collaboration. All of these skill categories are exercised in the most meaningful of ways as a key word program takes hold and gains steam. Among others, specific Language Arts standards for kindergarten state that the student will:

- Demonstrate understanding of the organization and basic features of print.
    (a) Follow words from left to right, top to bottom, and page by page.
    (b) Recognize that spoken words are represented in written language by specific sequences of letters.
    (c) Understand that words are separated by spaces in print.
    (d) Recognize and name all upper- and lowercase letters of the alphabet.
- Know and apply grade-level phonics and word analysis skills in decoding words.
    (a) Demonstrate basic knowledge of one-to-one letter-sound correspondences by producing the primary sound or many of the most frequent sounds for each consonant.
    (b) Associate the long and short sounds with common spellings (graphemes) for the five major vowels.
    (c) Read common high-frequency words by sight (e.g., *the, of, to, you, she, my, is, are, do, does*).
    (d) Distinguish between similarly spelled words by identifying the sounds.
- Participate in collaborative conversations with diverse partners about kindergarten topics and texts with peers and adults in small and larger groups.
    (a) Follow agreed-upon rules for discussions (e.g., listening to others and taking turns speaking about the topics and texts under discussion).
    (b) Continue a conversation.

There is a reverberating theme in these indicators. Early childhood standards demand that children's own lives be embraced into their school literacy experiences. Absent personal connection, the decoding skills of young children will fall upon a mere staccato of word mimicking. It is the enterprise of personal connection that is entwined with the expectation-laden skill of *comprehension*, that ultimate dimension of literacy development in which meaning is made.

INCLUSION NOT MARGINALIZATION

Worthy early learning literacy models begin with the idea that children have something to say and that reading and writing are channels of expression into and out of their own worlds. However, as with other curricula in which creativity and expression play a pivotal role, there has always been the danger that *key words* become an enrichment literacy playground of the privileged and entitled, leaving traditionally marginalized children in the lurch of robotic drill and skill lessons bent on remediating so-called deficit educational upbringings.

Key word work is harder to find in schools with significant bilingual populations, or in inner-city classrooms made up of children of color, or in programs that serve those euphemistically labeled as eligible for free and reduced lunch. Rather than ameliorating the achievement gap, this disallowance of a motivating language enterprise only feeds into disproportionality and the gap between well- and underserved students.

To teach literacy with integrity requires that a teacher demonstrate cultural relevancy and equity literacy. Much attention is paid to equity literacy in the pages that follow. Chapter 5 is devoted to the cultural context of doing key words.

At the same time, readers of professional literature are quite naturally going to wonder about how suggestions that populate the pages of any text might fit into the programs that they facilitate every day. Succeeding chapters, especially Chapter 4, make the case that there are natural harmonies to be found between common and approved reading and writing programs and this approach called key vocabulary. Methodologies of all sorts can welcome the activity of key words into their systems.

An urgent investigative pathway is to discover how marginalized children take to the idea of getting their own words. How do children in bilingual kindergartens and first grades experience the process of deciding for themselves what key words are added to their rings when it is time for doing words? This book offers many examples of real classroom sessions revolving around key word work. Many of the children who are the core of these stories are

English language learners, children of color, and other children outside of the dominant white, middle- to upper-middle-class culture. They are all enrolled in public school. And they have taught their teachers more than ever could be imagined about doing key words in the early grades.

NOTES

1. Ashton-Warner taught many four-year-olds as well, and the precepts about key words most assuredly can be practiced in pre-K programs.

2. Nina Zaratoga and Eric Dwyer, *Look I Made a Book: Literacy in a Kindergarten Classroom* (New York: Lang, 2005).

3. Regie Routman, *Reading Essentials: The Specifics You Need to Teach Reading Well* (Portsmouth, NH: Heinemann, 2003).

Chapter 2

Roots and History

Sylvia Ashton-Warner's story is a complex melodrama of unexpected twists and turns. It is grist for gritty screen writers, and in fact one of her autobiographical novels (*Spinster*) saw a Hollywood-style production (replete with Shirley McClaine in the starring role). Although the movie was hardly a success, the renown that Ashton-Warner gained as an educator and as an artistic writer is almost unheard of in the annals of public school elementary grades teaching.

This narrative stands as a convergence of the post–World War II progressive, idealistic era in education and the life course of an exceptionally creative, eccentric teacher who found herself at the nexus of indigenous children, a colonizer's education system, and her own impassioned yearning for meaning, truth, and artistry. Her life of teaching was often in turmoil, but out of it blossomed the DNA of what these days enjoys the appellation of *child-centered curriculum*.

Ashton-Warner was an innovator of pedagogical notions of individualization, creative curriculum, emergent literacy, cultural relevancy, and parental involvement. She is most definitely a member of the early childhood education hall of fame.

A STUBBORN SECRET: RELEVANCE

As a school teacher trained in the British tradition, at first Ashton-Warner organized her assignment in a Maori primary school by obliging young *Pipiriki*[1] students to grapple with readers and basals right out of the English school house. What she witnessed was a class of disinterested, disconnected children who made little progress as early and emergent readers. In letter that she wrote to her husband in 1940 she bemoaned that:

> there's no communication ... you see they're not thinking about what they're writing about or what I'm teaching. I'm teaching about "bed" and "can" but they are thinking about canoes and grandfathers and drowned men and eels. It seemed *rude to intrude*.[2]

The curriculum, as it were, was centered on sets of *Janet and John* readers, which were the British Empire's equivalent to the *Dick and Jane* books so ingrained in the cultural memory of North American grade schoolers. Imagine a series taking up the adventures of children in knickers kicking a ball, and such an image instantaneously captures the story line of these texts.

Ashton-Warner suspected *a stubborn secret*[3] as she hit the pedagogical brick wall of trying to teach word recognition through the use of this material. Though today it might seem a simple truth having to do with cultural relevance and learning, it was at that moment an elusive and agitating question. One student who attended this school had the following recollection about the curriculum imposed:

> I can't remember doing any Maori stories though, or anything to do with Maori at all. The education we got was strictly Pakeha;[4] Maori education—nothing. I can't even remember singing Maori songs at school.[5]

FEAR AND LOVE

It is not mere romanticism to conjecture that Sylvia Ashton-Warner became the discoverer of an insight about relevant literacy because her life was a jumble of introverted (and love-starved) psychological yearning, broiling artistic passion, as well as clear-eyed kid watching and zealous empathy. She also exhibited early in her career an *against the grain* predisposition. She distrusted bureaucracies and officialdom.

The children she worked with possessed inner lives that were so disconnected from their organized schooling that they were infantile expatriates when they returned to their own neighborhoods. At the same time, their collective consciousnesses were awash with internal imagery that was electric with affect. Their psychological development was bound by the drives that mattered for living and for learning—fear and love. When they saw words that evoked imagery about these emotions, the markings on the page flew off the paper and affixed themselves to concepts preexisting in children's minds.

Ashton-Warner's students quickly learned the words and that such manuscript forms meant something consistently. This secret and this discovery formed the starting place for Ashton-Warner's seminal book about facilitating the art of reading: *Teacher*.

ORGANIC READING

The discovery of key words led to the development of a system for teaching reading that Ashton-Warner called *organic reading*. Here is an important point to acknowledge, for every reading teacher understands that the learning process of *breaking the code* entails both the construction of a knowledge skill base and a way to go about making sense of all this new stimuli. It has to be organized so that it can be owned and embraced, while also becoming cognitively accessible. Reading is very much about creating internal organizational structures. For this reason, Sylvia Ashton-Warner cultivated her organic reading methodology not merely as a one-to-one learning transaction, but also as a way of setting up early childhood curriculum.

In order for a key vocabulary to reveal itself, children must be participating in a community of expression that gives permission for the inner world to emerge. Ashton-Warner very much believed that the human (and therefore the child's) psyche consisted on an inner and an outer world. The inner life was so much more interesting and revealing.

Thus, it was that every school day included a period of time devoted to creative expression. For an hour per day, her four-year-olds had at it with clay or paint in hopes of unlocking that inner world. This was called the *output* phase of the daily schedule. Most probably every day was different, and each session brought with it surprises and even outbreaks of emotion, but for the most part these sessions were intense with the creative workings of children. An atmosphere of peace abounded, not of hushed meditation, but rather the deep "lost within oneself" channeling of affect and concentration.

In the later permutation of her work, this time in the culturally uncanny land of 1970s middle-class, permissive, open-school baby boomer Colorado, she once again instituted this block of time as the *output* period of the school day.[6] It was a time for making and creating, and consisted of access to clay, water, blocks, dramatic play props, paint, and the works.

Although such a materially rich, child-centered environment seems standard from today's perspective, it was progressively innovative in the decades right after World War II, and it was very much a testimony to the advances of the field of psychology in a modern world. Children were a mishmash of emotional hullabaloo. They were the living embodiments of needs, egos, attachments, longings, aspirations, desires, fears, and anxieties. The classroom could be a window into this panorama of feelings, if they were encouraged to present themselves.

A good example of this was a series of infamous injection lessons Ashton-Warner set up prior to inoculation season. "[Sylvia] provided syringes to play with and apples to plunge the needles into."[7] In a sense, the children were inoculated against the palpable fear when youngsters have to get shots.

In fact, Ashton-Warner recognized fear as one of the two preeminent emotions. The other was love. She believed these were the two drives that contended in the affective world of the prelatency child. These passions were creatively attached to the imagery that was the communicative and expressive language of preliterate people. The artifacts were drawings, painting, clay forms, and conversational revelations that at the right moment could also receive a tag board word card written down. That was a key word.

> The key words carry their own illustrations in the mind, vivid and powerful pictures which none of us could possibly draw for them—since in the first place we can't see them and in the second because they are so alive with an organic life that the external pictorial representation of them is beyond the frontier of possibility. We can do no more than supply the captions.[8]

THE IMPORTANCE OF CHILDREN'S TALK

Child talk was the essence from which this pedagogy took form. An Ashton-Warner classroom was an environment where the students talked a lot, to each other, to the teacher, and among themselves. There was a dynamic din of chatter much of the time. It is worthwhile to contrast this atmosphere with the whole idea of "talking" as a pedagogical issue in kindergarten. The history of talking presents a schizophrenic value system in the annals of primary grades evolution as a rational educational approach. Much collective memory would attest to the fact that the early grades are all about learning not to talk—talking gets you into trouble. *Listening skills* stand for a classroom standard measured by a child's ability to sit and listen while the teacher talks.

Against this backdrop of behavior management and learning how to be a student in school, there is now the conflicting recognition that language development is both a receptive and an expressive enterprise.[9] As *performance* has been enfranchised as a hallmark of achievement, there is an indisputable recognition that for children to learn they have to be able to talk.

LEARNING CENTERS

A common solution to this paradox has been the elevation of learning centers as a traditional structural necessity in the modern ECE classroom. Learning centers fulfill the developmental exigencies of *initiative* and *industry*, which according to Erikson are two penultimate psychological dispositions that describe children four to six years of age.[10] Learning centers are also that time during the school day when students are free to talk. In an exquisite turnabout that flips the teacher's role on its head, this erstwhile classroom manager's job then becomes one of listening—to listen constantly, consistently, keenly, and purposefully.

Much of this behavior of teacher listening is ascribed to the purposes of assessment, which is the rallying call of modern ECE, but Ashton-Warner would most likely trumpet the fact that a teacher with sharp ears can hear the words spoken by each child that are key and precious to their inner world. She might not have labeled such classroom structure as learning centers per se, but the essence of child-centered activity would be the same. Chapter 4 addresses the *good fit* that exists as teachers consider including a key words component to the learning and literacy centers that have been mainstays in so many classrooms.

KEY WORDS COME TO AMERICA

All of these Ashton-Warner discoveries materialized out of her assignments in the 1940s and 1950s as a teacher of Maori children in New Zealand. With time, word began to get around, and her reputation found some germinating seeds. This style of teaching was raising eyebrows within educational agencies in Great Britain, and, more importantly, Sylvia's own writing was gaining a steady and growing readership. The first printing of *Spinster* sold out quickly, and after Simon and Schuster picked it up, sales shot up to 20,000 copies. *Time* magazine rated it one of the ten best books of the year. *Teacher* was published in 1963 and it became a hit with the American reading public. Although reception was quite a bit cooler in her home nation of New Zealand, Ashton-Warner was, on the basis of her writing and her reputation, an international figure.

This developing renown saw Ashton-Warner become elevated to possibly the most famous teacher of her day. Individual teachers rarely gain celebrity beyond the annals of educational bureaucracy, but this teacher's innovations made their way into newspaper features and the pop culture eye, and her writing was in high demand.

She was invited to lecture, and to model her approach internationally.[11] The stories of her worldwide circuit are scholarly captured in the biography *Sylvia!* by Lynley Hood, who makes it clear that fish bowl fame and the stress to perform were not always exact fits with this psychologically complex, some might say, neurotic, artist-teacher. In fact, one of the biography's chapters is entitled *Escape*, a summary term that reflects Ashton-Warner's deep and sometimes actualized desire to run away.

Nevertheless, it was in 1970 that the Aspen Community School, situated in the thick of the Colorado Rockies, invited Sylvia Ashton-Warner to become the lead teacher of five-, six-, and seven-year-olds at its new, exceptionally progressive and experimental place of learning. This year of teaching (and escape as well) resulted in the writing and publication of her simultaneously poignant and hilarious best published-in-America chronicle, *Spearpoint*.

The lessons of the *Spearpoint* saga are multitudinous, perhaps starting with the verification that key vocabulary (KV) can be culled and inveigled from all kinds of different student groups, in this case the offspring of the 1960s generation. Ashton-Warner called them the wannadowanna children and painted a picture of an indulged brood of progeny brought up on a theory of autonomy for the individual, leniency in discipline matters, and nonresponsibility for, or even any recognition of, the collective or community well-being. For example, Ashton-Warner's beginning-of-the-year attempt (with kindergarten and first graders) to set up a classroom jobs protocol resulted in the following exchange:

(Irritated [student]): I said I dowanna job. I don't have to. I can do what I like.

Ashton-Warner: Really!

Student: A- huh

Ashton-Warner: Interesting. I suppose you've brought your servants with you.[12]

In due time, Ashton-Warner learned that she would have to take a tack qualifiedly different from what she had used in New Zealand. As much as *Spearpoint* is about how American children slowly took to and embraced a key word approach, it is also about how a teacher must adjust pedagogy to the culture she finds in a school.

The book chronicles the pathway from children's resistance and rebellion in the wake of anything at all academically formal, all the way to their industrious production of stockpiles of key words, many of which would find their way into the sentences and booklets of writing that followed. Ashton-Warner wrote that while "some say dowanna, but key words cannot but endure."

Some of Ashton-Warner's travails in this brave new world of TV and media-saturated, consumerist, and autonomy-driven child development is reflected in the writings of Katie Johnson, whose book *Doing Words* is a treatise on applying a key word program into the context of American public school kindergarten and first grade. In both cases of Ashton-Warner's Aspen School experience and the rural Maine school story of Johnson's teaching of literacy, a significant permeating wonderment is an agitation about locating the inner life of children that is the floodgate of crucial (and key) vocabulary.

Given that fear and love are the two affective springboards that gush forth a KV, both of these chroniclers found themselves confounded by the materialistic and emotionally distant personas that inhabited their classrooms.

With Maori children, the regular and dependable first words were *Mom*, *Dad*, and the child's name. In Colorado, Ashton-Warner became used to the love cathexis as showered upon family pets. "Dogs are obviously key words," Ashton-Warner's bemusedly surmised.[13]

In her autobiographical last book *I Passed This Way* published in 1979, Ashton-Warner ascertained a "redistribution of instincts" as she tried to analyze how fear and love found themselves moderating into more placid affect. Key word work must evolve, she postulated,

> which is the magic of the key vocabulary—it accommodates itself to any state of mind, any variant of the mind, any culture, any race; in a cave or on its way to space.[14]

KEY WORDS IN THE TWENTY-FIRST CENTURY

The challenge for our current educational era, in the post–No Child Left Behind, Common Core–immersed, scientifically evidenced success landscape, is to channel this key word history into a methodology that captures the preciousness of children's KV while loosening the constraints of what is or is not key. There is an ambiguity about some words or captions that suggests there is a story surrounding any given object or item mentioned, even when a word does not seem to explode with that fear or love quality unearthed by the early theorists.

For example, what is a teacher to make of the occasion when six-year-old Israel, rather than asking for the word *pizza*, took the initiative to procure a new card, announce he would write it on his own, and proceed to form the letters *z a p p i* ?

Here is an opportunity fecund with phonemic stimuli and the potential to cement a critical epiphany about the way sequence determines lexicon. At the same time, Israel had just authored his own writing for meaning, displaying no small measure of self-efficacy—namely, if you know the letters, you can write anything. All of this accomplishment was duly and appropriately acknowledged while Israel worked on a new card that spelled the word correctly.

In the middle of tracing, copying, and illustrating the word, Israel blurted out the story that coated the word. "My baby sister ate pizza for the first time." This pronouncement came with a sincere facial expression as if to say "you have heard some monumental news just now." At times, *pizza* might be a hum drum word; in this case, the imagery-laden and inside-out power of this word *pizza* was evident, even though on its own merits it's just what one has for lunch.

The common thread through all words on a child's ring is ownership. The words emanate out from the child, announced, requested, or discovered through play or activity. The power and preciousness of key words bespeak ownership and the self-efficacy of claiming such a vocabulary.

SYLVIA ASHTON-WARNER'S UNINTENDED LESSONS

Sylvia Ashton-Warner wrote nine major books, six of them fictionalized, as well as the memoir-like nonfiction classics, *Teacher* and *Spearpoint*. Toward the end of her life, amid the ravages of alcoholism, family tragedies and health crises, and acute personal self-doubt, Sylvia Ashton-Warner wrote *I Passed This Way*, a 499-page autobiography. It soars to the same artistic heights she had staked out in her prime as a writer.

Her life inspired two definitive works by others that capture so much of the Ashton-Warner mystique: the biography entitled *Sylvia!* and a reflective testimonial entitled *Pay Attention to the Children*,[15] which transports wisdoms from this iconic educator up to a more modern time.

Scouring the history of such a provocative character unearths a subsequent set of unintended lessons from the Ashton-Warner saga that must be gleaned from the context and consequence of her teaching. These lessons are sublime and serve as complementary revelations in conjunction with the KV principle that has always been Ashton-Warner's penultimate contribution to the field of early childhood education.

Not every one of these lessons is laudatory. What is required is a reflective stance that counts on critical thinking and allows for the advancement of understanding that takes advantage of a twenty-first-century vantage point looking back on this mid-twentieth-century icon.

OFF THE PEDESTAL

A first caution is to acknowledge the pitfalls of the pedestal. Something to be avoided is putting individuals or methods on a pedestal, as such adulation becomes contrary to the goals of serving children and families well.

Sylvia Ashton-Warner's story is one of endurance of and resistance to a bureaucratic world. Teaching against the grain culminated in a legion of followers and near-hero status. Teachers might achieve prestige within their schools or communities, but rarely does a teacher gain celebrity status. People don't become teachers to be famous; children are taught *by* highly qualified personnel, not *about* luminaries in the profession.

Ashton-Warner chose an artist's path, and in so doing she elevated life in the classroom to something that could be dramatized and made into the subject of literary themes. Her first widely read novel *Spinster* forged new literary ground and was received with critical acclaim; additionally, it most surely did forge genre-shattering ground.

In *Spinster*, not only is the protagonist a classroom teacher of young children, the scheme of organic reading and KV is painstakingly chronicled within this work of fiction. The teacher, Anna, comes to an epiphany about KV that is imbued with drama. To some, it was the best novel to come out of New Zealand in the twentieth century. When *Teacher* was released, Ashton-Warner was propelled into the international spotlight. She was widely sought after and seemingly untouchable. Even after much of the Aspen Community School tenure had brought about fiasco-like incidents, the pedestal was still of worship proportions. Lynley Hood put it well in her biography: "Criticizing Sylvia Ashton-Warner in the 1970s was as unthinkable as criticizing Mother Theresa of Calcutta."[16]

But Ashton-Warner was from the beginning a troubled soul. She had a well-documented nervous breakdown in her late twenties, having found the monotony and self-sacrifice of motherhood just about unbearable. In these years, she became a child herself, a self-appellation that she hung onto in some form throughout the rest of her life.

She was eccentric and charming. She filled a room with her larger-than-life personality. At its best, this effervescence would cause others (a guest or new acquaintance) to feel special, honored, and esteemed when they had the good fortune to meet her or become a colleague. But some questioned Ashton-Warner's authenticity and took her demeanor as putting on airs. She could be pretentious. She was also known to turn on people—possibly a function of her low self-image. Lynley Hood summarizes the paradox as follows:

> The potency of her ideas, and her astonishing power to polarize her audience, lives on beyond her death. At the mention of her name, down-to-earth people turn misty-eyed with adoration, and mild-mannered individuals explode into rage.[17]

Teachers intuitively recognize that the children in their presence, though perhaps only four or five years of age, are indescribably complex people, with mood swings, fragilities susceptible to family events, and personality traits that contradict one another. The same portrayal can be associated with celebrities who have shaped pedagogy discourse. Putting someone on a pedestal diminishes the options to exercise critical thinking about his or her work.

When a theorist's design unfolds differently than was promised, there might be a tendency to dismiss that particular school of thought, but a more effective method may be to glean what is useful from their ideas and acknowledge the faults as well. In the classroom, teachers must adopt an attitude that innovations occur through the efforts of collectives of people, rather than by the actions of one leader.

DISCIPLES

Once she had arrived in North America, Ashton-Warner nurtured a bevy of adulating followers, some of whom became close friends. Her escape in the wee hours of the morning from the Aspen situation was carried out by the conspiratorial accomplice of some devoted people. The years immediately following Aspen provide the context for another unintended lesson especially germane for teachers thinking about the big picture.

After leaving the Aspen school, Ashton-Warner secured a position as a professor of education at Simon Frasier University in Vancouver, BC. She found herself before an audience craving insight to the secrets of early literacy. Throughout her professional life, she exhibited a love-hate tension between enjoying the classroom and a disdain for teaching, but at the university she was generally buoyed by convening the unique and remarkable adult class sessions that made up her university courses. This phase of her life leaves open the question of whether Ashton-Warner self-identified as an educational leader and authority, and if she had a mission to change the way early education was done.

Contradictory clues are scattered within her autobiography and writing. Having completed a successful year at Simon Frasier, those closest to her undertook the frustrating task of talking her into vying for a reappointment for another year. They were met with some typical Ashton-Warner roguishness. "I'm not interested in education,"[18] she recalled saying. That pronouncement came from this iconic figure who had been "ranked as one of the great educational innovators of the century."[19] Lynley Hood, Ashton-Warner's biographer, goes on to ask, "What was her cause?"

Ashton-Warner did, in fact, sign up for a second year at Simon Frasier, but it was not in order to lead the charges forward on a mission to reform infant education. To the argument made by colleague Tony Vogt, "You could help children through a university," she retorted, "I'm not crusader material, Tony."

What explains this apparent paradox and wherein lay lessons for teachers grappling with the pressures of an educational career in today's world? Conveniently and ironically, a hint of an answer rests in a word that almost certainly would rank as a key word for Sylvia Ashton-Warner in the heyday of her career: *espousal*. She used this word to encapsulate the profound, almost mystical harmony that comes about when children were submerged into their community of learners rapping out "*Tall* and *Wild* and *Grand* words."[20]

In her acclaimed book *Teacher*, Ashton-Warner concluded the chapter entitled *Life in a Maori School* by exclaiming, "I teach through espousal."[21] She was alluding to the integration that happens when there is common purpose inside a productive classroom—a union between learner and teacher. A synonymic phrase could be *the co-construction of knowledge*.

Espousal also connotes taking up a cause. It is the act of a teacher linking with something greater than herself, escaping the loneliness of being self-contained in a classroom and connecting with a bigger picture. Loneliness is a theme in the corpus of this artist/teacher that has been perhaps overlooked in deference to the many other major themes the story of her life invokes. Interestingly, she said of writing that it was the beginning of loneliness, an attribute she also ascribed to teaching. Espousal could have been an antidote.

As a revered professor at Simon Frasier, Ashton-Warner held court with her disciples, and there are tales of mesmerized protégées literally at her feet. The challenge was to take the theory, so in sync with progressive, open-classroom, organic approaches gaining credence in the 1970s, and move to some trials of implementation beyond the teaching she herself had already done.

One of these protégé relationships spawned the initiative to take organic reading ideas into classrooms of the Vancouver elementary school system. This initiative was named the Vancouver Project. A systematic plan was put in place to identify schools, classrooms, teachers, and student teachers who would integrate the KV method into their literacy programs. In the end, nine teachers from different schools, all working with children ages five to seven, took on the curriculum—all the while providing mentorship to carefully selected interns.

The story and assessment of the Vancouver Project are chronicled in an article entitled *Key Words: Impact on Reading*[22] written by Selma Wasserman, who became one of Ashton-Warner's close friends and confidants.[23] Ashton-Warner was typically initially amorphous in enthusiasm, but ultimately endorsed and was a supporter of the Vancouver Project. One of the criteria for being selected as a teacher was enrollment in Aston-Warner's seminars during the summer. The project proved to be successful on several counts, especially with regard to positive attitudes children expressed about reading and school in general. Additionally, the teachers-in-training who participated planned to take organic reading into their own classrooms as they moved on in the profession.

The art and science of learning to read is the stuff of unending discourse and debate. The topic is controversially political in the passions that are aroused. Given that reading level is equated with one's potential to be successful, and that failed literacy instruction has been a tool of dominant cultures to suppress marginalized groups, teachers are inescapably positioned as practitioners with profound connection to the most crucial of sociocultural matters. In other words, the implications of how the practitioner performs her craft extends well beyond the self-contained realm of a roomful of twenty-five children.

Ashton-Warner was not always a model of collegiality or an agent of change. But her promotion of espousal rings true. An unintended lesson for teachers in the twenty-first century is that union, integration, and advocacy all fall under the egis of this most compelling of key words: espousal.

Teachers have been described as *cultural workers*.[24] The use of this term suggests that whether intended or not, aware or not, teachers are fundamental transmitters to future generations about the ways things are done and what to value. In preschools, kindergartens, and primary grades, serious epistemological questions abound. The Sylvia Ashton-Warner legend contributes to the narrative that the way the basics are taught has profound connection to the major questions facing a society.

EVALUATING CONTEXT

Appreciating and appraising context is a necessary and lesson-laden activity that can only serve teachers well. It is especially imperative when tracking the relationship of Ashton-Warner with the Maori communities she lived among and the children she taught. What is the contribution of the Ashton-Warner story to current teachers' development as anti-racist, equity-literate educators?

There is much to unpack in this tale of a white New Zealander educator foraying into the realm of a colonized and indigenous people. The epiphany about KV that made her famous had everything to do with cultural relevance. Sydney Clemens' tribute to Ashton-Warner entitled *Pay Attention to the Children*[25] provides a reprint from a *Janet & John* primer reader that was the default basal found in Maori classrooms at the time Ashton-Warner was just beginning as a teacher.

It is a vivid and frankly comical representation of the misfit between British-based instruction and the lives of the children showing up in the classroom. The disconnect between British-based instruction and the lived experience of the students served as the agitation that harped at Ashton-Warner. It was what the protagonist in *Spinster* perseverated about until she hit upon her pedagogical revelation: a KV.

Yet the subtle ruminations of colonial and cultural racism are dimensions of the Sylvia Ashton-Warner story that are not to be ignored. The ultimate goal of her literacy curriculum was to transition "uncultured" children into the texts of the dominant world. As she noted in her autobiography, "The issue is simply the transition of a Maori at a tender and vulnerable age from one culture to another, from the pa to European education."[26] There is an assumption and transparent paternalism in the belief that cultured reading happens only when indigenous children are assimilated into the colonial mainstream.

The stereotype of Maori youth as riddled with violence—unruly, ancient warriors plagued by a technocratic modern era—is a thread through much of the Ashton-Warner corpus. The supposed chaos that is evoked is something she actually had an affinity toward, and in fact she couples this supposition of chaos with the motif of a living classroom. Ashton-Warner said of herself, "I am white on the outside, but brown on the inside."[27]

Such a pronouncement belies a privileged position that assumes it is possible to appropriate cultural dispositions and tamp down the social capital that is beneficed upon someone as an imprimatur of his or her racialized position. Ashton-Warner's story of growing up so very poor, yet the child of a teacher and the beneficiary of a system that would shepherd her through teacher training, is an instructive metaphor for the way power and dominance become recreated from generation to generation.

The following passage from *I Passed This Way* is revealing for the analysis she fell prone to:

> White children are the casualties in the Maori School context. You still hear about the arrogant pakehas[28] drawing the colour line but you want to see who draws the colour line when the Maoris are in the majority, from the Maori teachers down.[29]

Here is a reverse-discrimination argument based on supposed white minority status that could easily be heard in a teacher's lounge today. There is a logic embedded in such an observation that assumes that the psychology of solidarity that may culminate in what looks like a color line created by a group subject to colonization is the same and synonymous with an invisibility perpetuated by the dominant group. Critical analysis of the asymmetry in such comparisons is a responsibility of all teachers.

NONCONFORMITY

Ashton-Warner's uncritical assumption of cultural superiority cannot be ascribed to lack of courage. In fact, her sangfroid eagerness to run against the grain was one of the characteristics that endeared her to an avid fan base. She became a symbol for standing up (or at least out) to authority. Here is one explanation about why the era of the early 1970s saw Ashton-Warner become a cult hero. A convergence of counterculture ideas and resistance to institutional stultification brought outcries for people-oriented and life-affirming initiatives.

Hierarchies were to be interrogated and dismantled. Into this fray came the invigorating image of a schoolteacher flailing swords at the windmills of bureaucracy and institutional education. The top-down supervision and policy structure of the New Zealand educational system was incriminated as one force responsible for Maori alienation from schools and the people who made up the personnel.

Specifically, Ashton-Warner consistently received undistinguished marks and reviews by her supervisors. Her teaching was unappreciated, and she was unrecognized—an untenable cross to bear for someone who craved love, and truth be told, hid unfathomable self-doubt behind the veneer of charisma and self-aggrandizement.

A final hidden agenda educator's lesson to be gleaned from her remarkable life is that teachers rise to the occasion. Perhaps the quality of rising to each day's challenges, unexpected turns, emergencies, and spontaneous teachable moments is a characteristic about teaching that is unheralded and unrecognized. Teachers are required to be *on* as a matter of course, a disposition that is so much an expectation that its etiology is rarely explored. Ashton-Warner's life is a sample that can be probed. Here was a woman who had suffered depression so severe that it immobilized her. Her compulsion to run away never left her side, and the story of her escape from Aspen was merely the ultimate carrying out of getaways that played out in her mind on many other occasions.

And yet, Ashton-Warner had a habit of rising to the occasion. There are anecdotes in her story that are legendary—remindful of Hollywood-type dramatizations of protagonists pulling themselves out of doldrums to orate with inspirational tones.

The epitome of this kind of legend is a story told by Lynley Hood in the biography *Sylvia!*. At the tail end of her Aspen fiasco, having finished the memoir *Spearpoint*, Ashton-Warner was ready and anticipating her next escape. However, she had agreed to give a lecture to the University of Colorado's Third Annual Reading Conference:

> At the sight of a thousand excited reading specialists, she turned desperately to (the conference organizer): "I can't go through with it! I can't go through with

it!" He took her arm firmly and steered her onto the stage, muttering through clinched teeth, "I've invested a lot of time and energy in getting you here. You're not backing out now."

After a hesitant beginning she organized a lively key vocabulary demonstration with a group of teachers acting as five year olds, and talked in her ethereal and metaphoric way about the mind of our child . . . and about the poetry and drama of her life. She was magnificent.

Later in the day she took a second session.[30]

For all the biographical warts and regrets that must be included in a Sylvia Ashton-Warner portrait, the ability to live in the moment, rise to the occasion, and jump on the express that is the daily voyage of classroom life—that is a lesson any teacher in any educational era can hold on to and be inspired to show up and teach their heart out—each and every day.

CONCLUSION

Teachers are not endowed with many histories of educators that can be pored over for inspiration, affirmation, or simply self-identification. The KV history, and especially the Sylvia Ashton-Warner drama, serves as a buoyant mirror for the trials and tribulations of navigating the uncertain world of school. Teachers must process the relationship of the training they have received in preservice programs with the realities they are confronted with inside their own classrooms.

Whether a component of training or not, teachers discover a yearning for relevance. The Ashton-Warner experience chronicles this aching to discover such a stubborn secret, and thus the notion of a KV glistened. What occurred was an early example of cultural relevance. It did not transfer seamlessly to a Western, American setting, but the core tenets held true, regardless of venue.

In addition to the many insights directly pronounced by Sylvia Ashton-Warner, there are important unintended lessons to be gained from her life and teaching. Teachers must be leery of pedestalizing—an uncritical hero salute that depletes full countenance of context and nuance with regard to educational theory. Innovations in education are not the product of one individual.

Undoing racism and equity literacy are critical imperatives for school communities in today's world. Teachers can benefit from examining and analyzing the Ashton-Warner experience as the story of a pioneering teacher yet embedded in a colonizing paradigm. At the same time, there is a lesson to be taken from this writer extraordinaire who put forward the concept of espousal as a self-doctrine for her own teaching and career.

NOTES

1. Ashton-Warner carried out several different assignments in different Maori school communities. Her work in Pipiriki is what is chronicled in her masterpiece book, *Teacher*.
2. Lynley Hood, *Sylvia!: The Biography of Sylvia Ashton-Warner* (Auckland, NZ: Viking, 1988), 91.
3. Hood, *Sylvia!*, 101.
4. Of European descent.
5. Hood, *Sylvia!*, 99.
6. Ashton-Warner's tribulations as a teacher of American children are captured both hilariously and poignantly in one of her later books, *Spearpoint*. It is a chronicle of the nearly Herculean task of fitting a pedagogy rooted in the round peg of inner Maori child life revelations into the square peg of white-middle-class, television-absorbed, discipline- and accountability-minimal children growing up in America.
7. Hood, *Sylvia!*, 118.
8. Sylvia Ashton-Warner, *Teacher* (New York: Simon & Schuster, 1963), 39.
9. Joanne Hendricks and Patricia Weissman, *Total Learning: Developmental Curriculum for the Young Child* (Upper Saddle River, NJ: Pearson, 2006).
10. Erik Erikson, *Childhood and Society* (New York: W. W. Norton & Co., 1950).
11. In her autobiography *I Passed This Way*, Ashton-Warner tells of a farming group "on the backlands of Argentina" who were making use of her most famous text *Teacher*, a translated-into-Spanish version to be sure. Absent key word cards, the teachers would etch children's key words on the ground—a natural slate board so to speak.
12. Sylvia Ashton-Warner, *Spearpoint: Teacher in America* (New York: Vintage, 1970), 27.
13. Ashton-Warner, *Spearpoint*, 96.
14. Sylvia Ashton-Warner, *I Passed This Way* (New York: Knopf, 1979), 429.
15. Sydney Clemens, *Pay Attention to the Children: Lessons for Teachers and Parents from Sylvia Ashton-Warner* (Napa, CA: Rattle OK Publications, 1996).
16. Hood, *Sylvia!*, 214.
17. Hood, *Sylvia!*, Epilogue.
18. Ashton-Warner, *I Passed This Way*, 476.
19. Hood, *Sylvia*, 176.
20. Ashton-Warner, *Teacher*, 211.
21. Ashton-Warner, *Teacher*, 213.
22. Selma Wasserman, "Key Words: Impact on Reading," *Young Children* 33, no. 4 (May 1978): 33–38.
23. Ashton-Warner also had a falling out with Wasserman, as was the case with several relationships throughout her life.
24. Henry Giroux, *Border Crossings: Cultural Workers and the Politics of Education* (New York: Routledge, 1992).
25. Clemens, *Pay Attention to the Children*, 30.
26. Hood, *Sylvia!*, 137.
27. Hood, *Sylvia!*, 91.
28. A person of European descent.
29. Ashton-Warner, *I Passed This Way*, 321.
30. Hood, *Sylvia!*, 211.

Chapter 3

The System

Bertha is an English Language Learners (ELL) kindergartner who has come to the key word table for the first time. How will child and teacher arrive at that first word, which gets the process going and captures the essence of a very special word? Some children find a seat at the key word table and immediately begin to handle and fidget with the hole-punches—an opening for the teacher to say, "It'll be great to punch your word card as soon as you've gotten your first word. What's that word going to be? That's what we're trying to think of."

Of course, simply asking "what will be your word today?" is the easiest and most direct route to get the ball rolling. For eager children, a *just asking* approach is the right call, and, if anything, the challenge is to narrow their list down to words that are truly key. Some kindergartners, once they know the system, do a gaze around the room, taking in the environmental print and searching for a word idea. While such words may make it onto a card, these are not often the invested words that hold the inherent worth upon which Sylvia Ashton-Warner based her theory.

Bertha was eager enough and waited both patiently and anxiously for a signal that it was her turn to get started. When a child first arrives at the key words station, it is often the best teacher step to provide a small bit of jumpstart background. For example, the teacher might say, "Try to think of a special word; a lot of times it's someone in your family, or something you like to play." That is how *Mom* crops up so often. It could be argued that the child was directed toward this choice, but *Mom* is the most key word of all for many young children just starting out in reading. True to the point, Bertha happily and eagerly threaded *Mom* onto her ring as her very first word.

As a testimony to her British old-school credentials, Ashton-Warner was known to have discarded periphery words that children did not automatically assimilate. She describes an ownership about the words that sparks excitement and a realization that reading comports intense meaning. As chronicled in *Teacher*, the words have come "from deep within."[1]

As teachers reference the sociocultural context of twenty-first-century early childhood classrooms, they are well advised that it is inappropriate to discard work produced by their students. The goal rather is to excavate for the words that have much importance. In the co-construction process of child-centered pedagogy, the task is to discover those words that are truly part of each student's key vocabulary.

The process for getting to these words is differentiated and depends on the individual child, the teacher, and how the classroom is structured. Rather than a formula or a literacy procedure script, it is best to keep in mind some principles about the art of teaching that are time-honored and maintain resilience through wave after wave of educational trends. One such principle is that teachers must know their children well.

Avery is a five-year-old kindergartner at a school in Seattle, Washington. She is Chinese and Laotian American, and she is picking up English at a steady second-language acquisition rate. She is bright and does exceptionally well with all of the kindergarten assignments that this class of young learners tackles each day. Avery is also very shy and quiet. It takes her a long time to build trust and warm to a new program or opportunity for engagement. The key word station in her class had been open and chugging along for weeks and weeks without a successful recruitment of Avery's participation. Every once in a while Avery would matter-of-factly be invited to join at the key word table, but without success. She would busily occupy herself with all kinds of learning materials that were available during this project time block, but the key word choice table was not accomplishing its enticing magic.

The challenge was to figure out a way to exploit a conversation with Avery as a pathway into key word discovery. Clearly, this required much trust building before there was hope of her committing to this literacy interaction. A useful paradigm that can be invoked in such a scenario is the *power on, power for, power with* analysis innovated by Betty Jones at Pacific Oaks Children's School.[2] An observant teacher noticed that Avery was quite adept at doing 100-piece jigsaw puzzles that she often tackled during choice time. In many circumstances, teachers themselves must be perceptive readers of children.

In Avery's case, what was to be read was the subtle and unspoken messages that are broadcast by the child. While deftly trying out puzzle piece fittings, perhaps an adult's presence was not appreciated, which would mean a teacher's graceful retreat to a more distant location. But on one particular day, no retreat was necessary. Avery merely continued her puzzle making, with an air of "These grown ups, what can a kid do!" pasted on her face. Slowly, teacher and child built a relationship over puzzles that included a lot of self-talk and under-the-breath mumbling along the way: "This white one looks like it might be part of the clouds." Child and teacher worked together, with comments thrown in every once in a while. Then one day, the time was right for the teacher to say, "I just have a feeling that 'puzzle' is going to be your first key word."

It still took almost another week, but one morning, unexpectedly and unannounced, Avery found herself sitting in the *on-deck* position at the key word table that was set up as a center choice station in the classroom. A low and matter-of-fact intonation teacher voice welcomed Avery to this learning station with the expostulation, "Great, your turn is next right after Diego hole punches his word." Expressionless, Avery waited until she was directly asked, "Shall we do *puzzle* as your first key word?" Teacher hand and pencil had practically started in the motion of lowercase *p* when Avery, with precise and even exaggerated enunciation, caught eye contact and said, *flower*, which, in fact, became her first key word of what would be an extensive collection.

A NEGOTIATED PROCESS

The process of key words is a revelation into the child's world and to the communicative play inherent in learning new things. Avery's venture toward being in charge of her first word suggests the layered texture of what is involved in this negotiated discovery of what will be a new word. Knowing the child well is a dialectic balanced between observed informational bits and each child's expansive and complex way of being.

When teachers speak of *differentiated learning*, they are frequently referring to calibrated skill level and perhaps information processing styles. But how often do classroom teachers have the chance to go deeply into the give and take of knowledge construction? That is what the process of *getting a new word* is all about.

As it turns out Avery ended up choosing *puzzle* as a word later on (her fifth, to be exact). Knowing that she could name her new words all on her own was an important safeguard she needed to make sure about. Her story also demonstrates that the co-construction nature of key words is a humbling experience. Not only do teachers have to know the child, they also have to know that there is always more to learn.

The enterprise of determining what will be a child's next word is multilayered and is infused with rich transactions. At its core, this dialogue serves as the teacher's communication to students that "I care about you; I am genuinely interested in you as a person." Five-year-old students don't frequently experience this depth of interest within school buildings, and it takes the first few key word sessions to set the framework that they themselves are the determiners of their key word content. When children understand that key words are a means to talk about their families and their lives outside of school, it can be a floodgate. Once it is open, there can be a cascade of key word material.

A SIX-STEP PROCESS

The examples chronicled above exemplify just a few of the ways a new word is identified during the key word process. *Getting a word* is at the hub of a key word session. It is the kernel or the meat of the lesson. It is the second in a six-step process that each student goes through when they come to the key word table. The steps happen in the following sequence:

1. Reading the ring
2. Getting a new word
3. Tracing/copying the word
4. Embellishing the card
5. Hole-punching the card
6. Adding the word to the ring

The first three steps demarcate the process by which words are identified and provided. The latter three can be thought of as key word maintenance. The following section provides a more detailed description of how the first steps proceed, and what considerations a teacher ought to take into account. Chapter 4 continues the story by considering how a key word system can fit into and is so conducive with early childhood education curricula that are well known, widely practiced, and firmly in place in so many classrooms. The process is recursive and it works like gears as children opt for new words; there is a self-generating energy, as the cycle gets ready for the next words to come. Ashton-Warner summarized the tone of it with the following reflection:

> It may sound hard, but it's the easiest way I have ever begun reading. There's no driving to it. I don't teach at all. There is no work to put up on the blackboard, no charts to make and no force to marshal the children into a teachable and attentive group. The teaching is done among themselves, mixed up with all the natural concomitants of relationship.[3]

READING THE RING

For those students who have been consistently involved in key word work, a trusty and personalized ring has become a prized classroom possession. On this circular metal clasp, there dangles a bunch of word cards—ten, or twelve, to begin with and upward toward forty as the school year progresses. When a student comes to the key word table, his or her key ring is retrieved from wherever it is stored—be it a line of hooks mounted at child level along the wall, or inside of individualized shoe boxes each decorated by the key word reader.

Near the end of a school year, the ring may be overflowing with forty or fifty cards. The teacher is provided with the opportunity to ask a child to read several chosen examples. The reason for picking any given word might have to do with a phonemic connection just studied in today's reading lesson, or it might be as a vehicle for inspiring more elaborate (Movement III) prose. The term *movement* is all about the student writing that emerges out of the key word process. Chapter 6 is devoted to writing, movements, and all that happens as children's key word rings get filled up and children move into sentence formation, creating paragraphs and actual stories.

One of the most joyful moments in the key word progression is when a child is first starting out and has only one or two words dangling on the ring. This is the exact time to set about the routine of reading the ring. When Amir arrived at the key word station for just the second time, he plunked down into the writer's chair and said, "I want *airplane*!"

"Such a great word!" the teacher replied enthusiastically. "Let's keep that in mind, but first" and with a finger pointed to one of the two words he had gotten in the first session, "What does this word say?"

Amir read both words on his ring, set it aside, and watched the word *airplane* get printed on a new card. In short order, his ring held a third word, and then a fourth, as the development of his key vocabulary was on its way.

Naturally, there are many opportunities for students to read their rings to each other. When three or four kindergartners are working at the same time, this is often a worthwhile strategy for on-deck people, while someone else has the teacher's full attention. Such partnering ensures lots of reading practice and also plants ideas for new words. Rarely does a student simply copy another's choices, but often a child is inspired to think in a new direction about meaningful and precious images.

In *Doing Words*, Katie Johnson describes the activity she implemented of claiming words.[4] After the key word input period had ended, each child with new words to add to their set, Johnson would gather all of the new cards, loosely shuffle them, and scatter them on the rug in the middle of the circle. Children enthusiastically scampered to claim their own, an activity sure to provoke an automatic convocation of literacy. Johnson's method can be compared to a procedure Sylvia Ashton-Warner described in which she posted new words on the board—a public celebration so to speak.

Teachers can be creative about other forms of key word games or activities that are ripe for invention in order to support a class community experience about these special kinds of sight words. It should be noted that such games serve the purpose of expanding key words into a bigger language experience. The essential specialness of key words always rests with the caption and inner-emotional life quality of the words themselves. With that caveat in mind, Christie, Enz, and Vukelich[5] cite the work of Jeanette Veatch, who was a disciple of Ashton-Warner and came up with the following extensions:

- *Retrieving.* With words scattered on the floor as described above, children in turn find a word and read it aloud.
- *Alphabet classification.* Words are recorded or posted according to their beginning letter. Newsprint poster paper labeled by letter can be used for this whole class activity.
- *Environmental word search.* "Children might find their key words in books, magazines, newspapers."

Given that the key word experience is rooted in the individual vocabularies and personalities of the children in a class, different children also bring idiosyncrasies to this first step of reading the ring.

When *grandma* and *abuela* were shared words among classmates, Rosa was quickly struck with the memory of her grandmother's *pajaro*. Without fail, Rosa wanted to read *pajaro* every time she worked on key words, and even when her ring was weighty with entries, her grandma's bird was an item to be read, reviewed, and remembered.

As students traverse through the succeeding movements, they have begun to write stories and narratives, and there is less attention to the ring of words that helped get it all started. Even so, it is worthwhile and a part of the ritual to go back and read some of the ring words each time. It can be a reflective moment for many children as they come to recognize how literally precocious they have become. They are able to track their progress and development in an organic way, much in keeping with the organic reading philosophy at the heart of doing words. Such visits to prior learning are also at the root of metacognition.[6]

GETTING A NEW WORD

The way Sylvia Ashton-Warner put it,

> First words must be already a part of the dynamic life. First books must be made of the stuff of the child herself, whatever and wherever the child.[7]

It is a marvel how quickly and easily both monolingual and bilingual children click into this activity of *doing words*—creating their own key vocabulary of word images that evoke special meanings of love, family, importance, and self-definition. All of the vital processes of learning are intertwined in these accumulated acts of getting new words. Children are constructing their own knowledge because they are veritably requesting to see and to know the literacy tags that are assigned to these most precious images. Such construction is happening at both a personal and social level, because the interaction that happens among peers exerts enormous influence on motivation and on the available tableau of experience that each student considers worthy.

The teacher is serving as facilitator and knowledgeable guide while also sustaining structure and expectations—but within the framework of a child-centered model that counts on the internal disposition of joyful rigor. And finally, the tasks within a key word session are naturally calibrated in order to line up appropriately in the *just right* range of each student's zone of proximal development.

In most early childhood classrooms, friendship is a major theme. This topic becomes central regardless of whether the teacher has planned a unit or set up a series of lessons about classroom community. When it comes to kindergartners and first graders, *my friends* are a central focus of the inner world.

Chelis was brand new in Marletta's kindergarten classroom on just his second day of school. He was content enough, but being a primary Spanish speaker in a sea of English cannot be easy. One day, Chelis encountered six-year-old Saulo who was enmeshed in Movement III writing (see chapter 6), meaning that he was well launched into a paragraph story that had evolved as an elucidation of one of his early key words. Chelis slowly meandered over to the key word table ready to start his own key word journey.

Although clearly curious about the workings of this center about words, Chelis was having a hard time tracking the English explanation of what was going on. Some inexact Spanish phrases (*palabras muy especiales*, *cosas importantes*) began the explanation, whereupon Saulo took a moment to interrupt his own work and embark on a complete and impressively adroit explanation in Spanish of what his classmate was supposed to do.

An air of understanding spread across Chelis' face and he named the word *chair*. Though probably not a "key" word, it was dutifully charted onto his first card, but before Chelis even got started on the exciting step of punching out the hole, he asked for his second word.

My friend—Saulo.

Saulo became Chelis' next key word, and *friend* was added soon thereafter. *Friendship* is a major theme in kindergartens whether the teacher plans it or not. It resonates with the inner world of the child.

CONVERSATION AT THE CORE

From the outset, conversation is at the root of key word interaction. The act of conversation has a creative dimension that is crystallized during key word sessions. In many ways, the process is much like artistic endeavor because the act is consistently one of following the creative process so that the word can be brought forth. Consider for a moment how Tanya arrived at knowing that *Mom* would be her next key word, to be followed by *Dad* and then *baby*. It all had to do with the fact that on one early October day, Tanya was ready to do key words and she was wearing a blouse with a small Winnie the Pooh emblem sewn in the front. Her teacher's first musing prompts were not successfully soliciting word ideas.

"Hmm . . . I wonder . . . what word will you get today . . . ?" Tanya remained unsure and uncommitted. In order to be silly and light, the teacher changed the pace by saying, "I almost feel like asking that bear who's on your shirt."

"That's Winnie the Pooh" was Tanya's retort, somewhat exasperated by this sign of adult ignorance.

"I know that story! My daughter used to have a stuffed Pooh bear when she was about your age."

Tanya thought a moment and said, "I got this shirt at Disneyland. My Mom and Dad took us."

"But I don't know if *Disneyland* or *Mom* or *Dad* is going to be your next key word."

"*Mom*, of course" was her assured response, although *Dad* followed in due course, and her brother Octavo, who was still a *baby*, became the third word she added to her ring on that day. Arriving at *Mom* in this way was special in a manner that would not have had equal significance were it simply to have been given to her as a word, out of context. Tanya was the one who had created the emotional caption.

Jim Cummins, one of the leading authorities on ELL and bilingual development, counsels that it is vitally important to engage young second-language learners in conversations.[8] Such interactions are called *context-embedded* activities; the trick is to be able to structure things inside of classrooms so that children move from cognitively easy tasks to cognitively demanding challenges. What remains constant is that the focus is about context-embedded, personally meaningful material. When conversation leads to writing, the challenge is increased and the context is held constant. How different from the cut-and-paste worksheets that are the mainstay of some kindergartens where children are just learning English?

A WORD—OR A PHRASE

Sometimes the output comes in the form of sentences and phrases—personal narratives, or the kind of captions teachers like to see as journal entries. For kindergarten and first-grade students, the line between a sentence and a word can be fuzzy, which provides the teacher with fecund opportunities to teach about language and structure within the context of meaningful content.

For example, during one of Melissa's first sessions at the key word table she thought long and hard about what word she wanted to ask for. Since she was new to the process, she was met with the usual succinct explanation of what students were doing and what is meant by *key words*.

As is typical of many children, Melissa paid lateral attention to classmates nearby and had begun her own formulation and construction of what was going on. Clearly, and especially on this particular morning, people's families were a significant ingredient; the door was open so to speak to share the funds of knowledge,[9] which every child brings into the classroom when the topic is family.

"Raul, he's my brother," Melissa offered at the moment she had gained teacher attention with a nonverbal signal that it was her turn to solicit help with a new key word. In such a case, options are plentiful with regard to how a teacher might proceed. It depends on deciding what the goal is at the moment. Cautiously, this teacher picked up on her pronouncement and replied,

"We could make *Raul* your next word, or maybe you would like *brother*. There's time today so you could get both of them as key words."

Confused, Melissa stared at the card and seemed a little miffed that the teacher pencil had not started its course of hieroglyphics across the middle so that she could follow with her task, which was to trace over the letters with her index finger. As if to accentuate that insufficient attention had been paid, Melissa merely repeated the cogent information.

"Raul, he's my brother."

"Let's write exactly that" thus became the perceptive acknowledgment, and *Raul he's my brother* was inscribed as Melissa's newest key word.

Kindergartners are asked to trace over the letters first with their fingers and then with a crayon. As Melissa did so, she was made privy to the following commentary.

"This is the part that says *Raul*, See, there's a space between the words. Let's find the word *brother*. That's the one that starts with the letter b."

In this way, phonological and grammatical awareness is easily built into key word interchanges.

Isaiah came to the key word table and burst out with the declaration that "I am five!" It is hard to represent in this written chronicle the verve and conviction behind his announcement. He was conjuring up the most important testimonial of information he possessed at that particular moment. Key words are about important matters. What is special? What is your word today? Isaiah would have as his word *I am five*. Herein is the affective bond at work, for surely this simple burst of a blurb instantaneously became an identity caption to be read over and over.

Isaiah's word that day was a phrase, and here too was an opportunity to break down the parts and analyze what was on the page in a supported and co-constructed way. In short order, Isaiah was primed to learn that "I am" has endless possibilities for more writing and that "I" itself is one of the really useful words in a reader's vocabulary. But for today, *I am five* became his word and after tracing and copying, he hole-punched it onto his key ring collection.

Ultimately, the goal is to inch all children in the class along the way to cataloguing phrases and sentences. Key word work is a developmental progression whereby new writers are bootstrapped into elaborated expressions on paper. Imagine, for example, the satisfaction a kindergartner might feel when the teacher, so filled with genuine delight, exclaims, "You didn't get just a word! You got a whole sentence!"

These thresholds become the transfer points in and out of six *Movements*. The construct of *Movements* was posited by Sylvia Ashton-Warner whose musical pedigree informed much of her other endeavors. The attributes and qualities of movements were more exactly codified by Katie Johnson whose treatise *Doing Words* provided an American point of view for the organic literacy approach. Children traverse in, out, and through these movements in a natural and organic way as their paper-and-pencil literacy takes hold.

Eventually, key word rings become stuffed with so many cards it's hard to keep track while the words themselves become dog-eared and lovingly tattered; word cards give way to stories and personal narratives, and the writer's medium transforms into booklets and journals. *Moving* is a good word to describe this progression because children are constantly moving upward into unfettered zones of development and teachers (as well as parents) are moved by their growth, their learning, and, of course, their stories.

TRACING/COPYING THE WORD

Once a word has been identified and written crisply on the front side of a key word card, there is the opportunity for the student to engage with the word by embellishing it with her own handiwork. It should be mentioned that there are various schools of thought with regard to this process; some teachers prefer to have their students simply collect their words without any manuscript production at all. From this standpoint, Movement I key word work is seen as entirely a reading enterprise where children's challenge is to know the words as formed by the teacher's pen. On the other hand, there is much value in giving the new word recipient an immediate task to do, once the look and form of the word have been contemplated and realized.

Educators often talk about the kinesthetic encryption of learning and the activity of tracing over the letters of a word sets up a neuron firing that helps cement ownership and sight memory. Novice readers might simply be asked to trace over the letters with their index fingers; more often than not, the next step is to trace with a crayon or colored pencil, thus gaining letter formation practice, while also invoking personal markings upon the paper. Economic teacher commentary easily accompanies this writing exercise—for example, "you traced a perfect 'p'" as the young writer follows the curves of the letters in *airplane*. Or, "Yes, Javendeep, that is the last letter in your name."

An advanced step beyond tracing is to copy the word underneath the teacher's writing, still on the front side of the card. Some children quickly go beyond the need to trace so that copying the word is the obvious and appropriate task. The step of copying is rich in assessment potential. The teacher is easily able to learn what letters are solidly in a student's schema and which are shaky. Assessment questions are such as the following: Does the student know the shape of the letter? Does the student know the name of the letter? And at a most basic level, is the student demonstrating one-to-one correspondence between the model and the copy? All of these items can be looked at in the context of naturalistic performance assessment during which the motivation factor is high.

Every teacher also knows that the range of penmanship competence and confidence is enormous. In any given kindergarten, there will be shaky pencil writers as well as budding calligraphers. Copying gives children a chance to see their own words in their own handwriting. It becomes an embedded lesson into the constancy and transference of word configurations. It is fascinating to watch the emergent reader focus on a card that possesses the teacher's writing as well as her own. "What does this arrangement of letters say?" It is the pattern and sequence of letters that takes hold and the student is well on the way to realizing a core secret about the code of reading: it is the order of letters that makes a difference, whether in a printed book, on a commercial flash card, or in the copied formation of a key word.

A new word appears on a card. The student has read her ring of words, conversed with the teacher, identified the new word, and copied it on a card. She will read this word often, and ultimately use it in expository writing. The next steps are maintenance steps, and they too contribute to feelings of specialness and ownership. These words are key, and they are keys to literacy.

CARE AND COLLECTION

One of the threads that run through all of the elements of key word work is the notion of *ownership*. Organic literacy rests on the idea that children's personal stamps and imprimaturs must be emblazoned on new words they are learning, and on the actual physical processes that go along with learning to read and write. Children invest through the selection of words and in the maintenance procedures that result in individual rings heaping with words. Although these technical steps do not offer measurable contribution to language arts skill acquisition, they are part and parcel intertwined with the positive dispositional trajectory that describes a key word curriculum.

These procedures can be named as the *care and collection* stages that follow word identification and new card creation. Children are participating in the creation of their own learning materials, invoking ownership as an investment in learning. After a student has received a new word card, finger-traced the letters, traced with a crayon or colored pencil, copied the word, and thoroughly taken in the word as a caption for something special and important, she is invited to embellish it according to her own wishes.

DRAWING AND EMBELLISHING

Alondra is a six-year-old in Mrs. Garcia's primary ELL class. A peek at her key word ring reveals the following: *Alondra, mom, dad, Mother's Day, walking stick, bike, computer, Father's Day, Today is Father's Day*. Most of the words are undecorated, but the small self-portrait sketch underneath her name *Alondra* captures the eye. It has the typical cartoonish form of circle head, eyes, and mouth worthy of all happy face smiley stickers, a box rectangle body, with arms and legs that protrude like sticks, and some exceptional hair.

This hair is not scribbles of strands or a Lucy-type shock of curl. Alondra's hair is a sweeping chiffon of hairdo, curled at both ends 1950s style with a line of form that follows the wave, giving the whole fashion body and depth. Whereas she drew her body about an inch tall under her name, the hair that sits on her body uses two inches of curved space. She drew the outline of herself and her coif in purple, with all of the hairstyle filled in green. Figure 3.1 shows the happy face smiling from ear to ear.

The distinctiveness of children's art certainly comes across in their key word illustrations. This option to add an illustration under the word or on the back side provides one more layer of engagement to the key word table. As mentioned earlier, some teachers caution against a feature that is artistic rather than literary, but integrated and cross-disciplinary curriculum theory heralds the infusion of visual arts (and all other kinds as well) into language arts lessons.

Figure 3.1 "Alondra's Coif"

This step allows for a more deliberative, tempo-laden session at the key word center. When three or four children are doing key words at the same time, each is involved in a different stage so to speak, and this ambiance takes on a tone quite akin to a veritable writer's workshop.

While other key worders are embellishing cards, the teacher can steer her attention in the most efficient direction, which generally means focusing on the point at which new words are identified and written. Children with a voracious appetite for lots of key words are paced by environmental signals that encourage them to take their time with each word. The ownership paradigm is revisited as an alternative to the quantified assembly line production model that has become typical of American classrooms.

Perhaps most importantly, this step of drawing and embellishment opens up the creative channels that keep motivation strong and make learning meaningful. Coupled with the emotional attachment to new and precious words come the child's personality-laden traits of artistry, cleverness, quirkiness, sense of humor, and self-constructed expression. As has been made famous by the architects of Reggio Emilia schools,[10] the world is enriched by the *hundred languages of children*. A few of them make their way onto the card stock of key words.

As will be discussed in chapter 5, names of friends populate the cards of many students who are given the opportunity to do key words. The point will be made elsewhere, but it is worth noting that an important community agreement is that a peer's name is used only after permission has been

Figure 3.2 Students embellish their key words

secured from the student in question. Names are sacrosanct; students must ask permission for them to show up in stories and on key word cards. Permission granted, they are certainly ripe for embellishment of all sorts. Figure 3.2 captures some examples of key word cards by students obliged to have some décor to go along with their printed letter forms.

HOLE-PUNCHING THE CARD

A key word center or table is stocked with key word cards, the necessary writing utensils of pencils, crayons, colored pencils, and markers, and a couple of well-maintained single-hole punchers. This tool is likely to be new to most kindergartners. It lives, so to speak, at the nexus of concrete operational child development for the five-year-old or even the early first grader. The physical action of punching a hole is a metaphoric seal of completion. It is as if to say, "There, I've received a new word; it is ready for filing."

At the same time, the squeeze feat of compressing the puncher through the card provides just the right level of motor challenge to take its place among the mini-rights of passage along a child's path to competence. Some kindergartners wield this tool with swagger and a carpenter's grip, while other five-year-olds are at first barely able to form a cardboard indentation with the pokey awl.

Such a small muscle developmental continuum calls upon the standard ZPD scaffolding tactics that teachers employ in any given skill development situation. ZPD refers to the term *zone of proximal development*, coined by Lev Vygotsky as a way of describing what a child is able to do with some assistance from a more accomplished person. It is a concept of extreme importance because it instructs the observer to think of skill level as a continuum rather than an up or down labeling.

The core principle is to help sufficiently in order to get the task accomplished, while receding and distancing enough so that the child has participated and exerted strength. Such diminishing is at the core of what teachers do when they are scaffolding learning. It is all in the service of the learner acquiring a more independent role. Much of the literacy approach called *The Daily Five* hinges on this *gradual release* model. In a general sense, teachers are gradually releasing responsibility for accountability and sustained attention to a task. Or, in the case of using a hole punch, the release is more kinesthetic, literally letting go of the metaphoric elephant's feather as the child achieves the task herself. See chapter 4 for a discussion of the Daily Five.

There is also a dimension of motivation. Anybody who has watched a young child snap a punched hole knows that the instinct is to want to do another one presto right away, which of course results in the need to think of a next and new word.

Dyandros is a five-year-old kindergartner with an overflow of spunk and energy. One recognizes a remnant of younger sensory motor stages of development in his busy and tactile manner of being in the world. His first foray over to the key word center was not so much an arrival as it was a plummet upon the material. Within seconds, a hole punch was in his hands, the paper a primed subject of attack. This kind of learning disposition requires a gentle hand interceding and controlling the metal utensil while simultaneously narrating the following bit of information:

> Dyandros, you are so ready to make a hole for your first key word. Let's get started thinking up what that word will be.

The rules for use of the hole punchers soon get established as part of a *doing words* protocol. The punchers sit safely in a box until the process has moved through the regular steps:

- Read the ring.
- Determine a new word.
- Have it written neatly by the teacher.

- Finger-trace and pencil trace.
- Copy.
- Embellish.
- Now punch.

And it is ready to be dangled onto the ring, taking its place next to all words that came before it.

The ritual of punching a hole in the key word card confirms the addition of a new word and adds to the one-to-one correspondence of new word officially inscribed on a new card, dutifully hole-punched, as if the train conductor had punched the ticket, now ready to be filed away.

ONE LAST STEP: THE RING

A key word card, freshly hole-punched, is carefully threaded through the silver key ring that is provided for each student. One of the best designs is the clawed snap ring with a hinge that comes undone with an opposite direction force exertion and a simultaneous spreading open of the two metal arcs joined at the pivot. This is another *no easy task* for the unsure fingers of five- and six-year-olds, and requires the same kind of individualized proximal assistance that teachers offer during hole-punching. These adult-like small motor accomplishments are frequently just challenging enough for budding primary grade children who are feeling their oats and exposing a bit of concrete operational superciliousness about their graduation out of the preschool years.

Sometimes kindergarten teachers intentionally design easily performable curriculums so as not to compromise tender self-esteems. Such care warrants a balance of hard jobs that require concentration and exertion. An "I can't!" or two may be heard at the key word table early in the year every now and then. Rarely does such a refrain last until spring. Even children who struggle with the ring-opening task have no trouble snapping the ring together. The word is safely lodged, and the ring can be returned to its shoebox home. The cycle of ownership is primed for the next go-around.

NOTES

1. Sylvia Ashton-Warner, *Teacher* (New York: Simon & Schuster, 1963), 49.
2. *Power on, power for, power with* stands for an observational analysis of interactions between an adult and a child, depending upon the degree of influence and exertion emanating from the more sophisticated actor. For example, when an adult simply tells the child where to place a puzzle piece, that is power on. The same adult might make a suggestion based on color which would be power for. When the

adult subtly and non-verbally slides a piece into view, she is practicing power with. These power concepts are very much in keeping with the Vygotskian notion of Zone of Proximal Development and scaffolding.

3. Ashton-Warner, *Teacher*, 49–50.

4. Katie Johnson, *Doing Words* (Ann Arbor, MI: Braun-Brumfield, 1997).

5. James Christie, Billie Jean Enz, and CarolVukelich, *Teaching Language and Literacy: Preschool through the Elementary Grades*, 3rd ed. (New York: Pearson, 2007).

6. It is now widely accepted that young children can think about and reflect on their own learning. The question of meta-cognition is taken up in chapter 4 as part of addressing how children understand the learning that goes on while doing key words. See Chatzipanteli, Athanasia, Vasilis Grammatikopoulos, and Athanasios Gregoriadis. "Development and Evaluation of Metacognition in Early Childhood Education."

7. Ashton-Warner, *Teacher*, 6.

8. Jim Cummins, *Negotiating Identities: Education for Empowerment in a Diverse Society* (Los Angeles: California Association for Bilingual Education, 2001).

9. *Funds of Knowledge* refers to the wealth of skill, experience, cultural background, and information that every family brings to a school setting regardless of formal education attainment level.

10. The Reggio Emila approach is renowned for the artistic heights that young children are able to achieve. At its core, Reggio Emila philosophy promotes the orientation that children are competent and capable, well beyond the expectations as they exist in many American ECE programs. See chapter 7 for a more complete discussion.

Chapter 4

Key Words
A Natural Fit

Primary grades classrooms have since time immemorial been divided into groups to which teachers allocate their attention differently—usually according to ability, named in some educational era or other as *bunnies, butterflies,* and *ladybugs*, or designated according to three continents, or christened according to three student-elected candy bars.

These group appellations have survived countless structural permutations and literacy modernizations, and yet one classroom management conundrum has beleaguered instruction designers from the days of one-room school houses all the way to the digital classroom. Whether students are working on slates or iPads, the question of teacher attention allocation has persisted.

Given that reading is an individual skill requiring the focused attention of the teacher in a one-to-one exchange, here is the rub: what occupies all the other students while the teacher instructs the low group, or the Response to Intervention group, or the highly capable group? What keeps them busy without the teacher's supervision?

This seminal structural question has to be coupled with a prime and singular quality about the key word enterprise: participation is based on student personal choice and internal motivation. It would be oxymoronic to attempt to tease out of a resistant or oppositional child words that project personal deep imagery.[1] Arrival at the key word table needs to be the result of choice and individual incentive. A child coerced to produce key words will play the game and parrot back teacher offerings, but the ownership emblematic of the transaction will be shallow and unfulfilled.

But when used adeptly, a key word program has every chance of drawing in the entire class, even the reluctant learners. The pivotal instructional measure has to do with structural design that honors and respects choice while centralizing key word work as worthy of student investment. Ideally, students can't wait for a chance to get to the key word table, because there is individual attention, they can go at their own pace, and the words are important. They might spark warmth, fear, or a story of some kind. What is immutable is that they are special.

The following four early childhood literacy models are offered here as high potential systems for incorporating key words in an integrity-driven way. They are not presented in these pages as way of promotion or advertisement. Rather, they stand as representative of how key words can naturally fit into set systems. They are examples that take their place among other approaches unified in recognition of a child-centered manner of child development.

The following four approaches will be discussed from the standpoint of how key words can fit logically into each one's overall design: The Daily Five, Early Learning Literacy Centers, Walk to Read, and HighScope. What is offered is not a comprehensive account of these time-honored and popularly adopted approaches to learning; rather, there is a broad overview portrayal with an emphasis on each one's adaptability in order to incorporate the enrichment that the key vocabulary system and experience is sure to provide.

KEY WORDS AND THE DAILY FIVE

The Daily Five (D5)[2] was authored intentionally as a management system bent on maximizing student engagement and ensuring that students were rigorously exercising and advancing their reading and writing skills during the blocks of time set aside for literacy learning.

There are several iconic idioms that come out of D5 theory and literature, and some of them conjure up organic reading terminology coined by Sylvia Ashton-Warner nearly fifty years previously. For example, authors Gail Boushey and Joan Moser ("The Sisters") beseech teachers to model an EEKK-paired reading posture in which learners sit *elbow-to-elbow, knee-to-knee* as an assurance of focused stamina-oriented engagement when the activity calls for students to read to each other, one of the five daily reading options. Ashton-Warner had a similar idea when she made the following observation as she purveyed the Aspen, Colorado, classroom in 1970:

> They would be reading now in groups of two or more the words of their own they've accumulated, talking about them, teaching each other knee to knee, hearing each other, spelling them, associatively discursive.[3]

One of the iconic concepts of D5 is the *sense of urgency*. While perhaps more stringent in tone than the naturalistic sound of organic reading, both philosophies evoke the child-centeredness and ownership of literacy that springs from the inner world. It is as if to say, this stuff of literacy *must* unfold! It is so important because *you*, as a growing participant in the literary world, *are so important as well.*

Key vocabulary work can seamlessly blend into the structure of D5 design. It is not hyperbole to say that *The Daily Five* and *Key Words* are a match made in child-centered, curriculum heaven. There are two components and two characteristics of the D5 approach to literacy that ensure this pedagogical harmony. The components are *choice* and *word work*. The characteristics are *gateways to writing* and *differentiation*.

CHOICE

The D5 is exactly what the name suggests: a system founded upon five enterprises that make up the literacy block in a classroom's schedule. Boushey and Moser call them tasks and this set of five has become fairly routine and sacrosanct in countless classrooms, K-3, and beyond. As named by "The Sisters," the tasks are *read to self, read to someone, work on writing, listen to reading,* and *spelling/word work*. During the D5 block in the school day, every student in the class is engaged in one of these five tasks, and they are all occurring simultaneously. A student may perform two or even three of these activities during the full block time span, which can range from half an hour at the beginning of the year to ninety minutes or more when all pedagogical cylinders are firing. How do the students know which ones they are supposed to be doing? They choose.

The subtitle of the original D5 text heralds *Fostering Literacy Independence*. A core value of the system is autonomous and motivated initiative to be immersed in the behaviors of reading and writing. At the root of fostering such independence is the opportunity, and in fact the responsibility, to make involvement choices among the five-option menu. In fact, this choice making process is an important moment in the D5 work block. Teachers become adept at manufacturing efficient choice-making routines, but each class member chooses one of the five on his or her own. Once a full class has registered its destination, D5 tasks commence.

WORD WORK

Every student has a choice of which task to tackle: read to self or to someone else, listen to reading, work on writing, or Word Work. This last task title is comprehensively inclusive of a wide range of activities that exercise phonics skills, sight word fluency, word families, spelling, handwriting, and grammar.

Boushey and Moser interchange the terminology of Word Work with the phrase *Word Study,* both of which denote the experience of immersing oneself deeper into the world of words. The nature of these tasks can vary from worksheet mastery, to *read the room* investigations, to spelling list practice using a wide variety of techniques. There might be a board game to play, or a manipulative set up to perform such as matching or classifying.

Word Work is the place to develop vocabulary, memorize irregularly spelled high-frequency words, master the sight word inventory that produces fluency, and practice the phonetic rules that are utilized as word attack strategies: The *e* does the talking and other phonic maxims. "The Sisters" proffer an exceedingly cautionary slice of wisdom about word work:

> During Word Work we focus on spelling and vocabulary work with children. There is considerable controversy about the best way to teach these. The Daily Five structure does not dictate the best method to use in teaching reading, writing, spelling, or vocabulary work, but instead creates a richly literate environment that provides essential and often-skipped practice time.[4]

Word study generates four enterprises that make up this choice in the literacy block: practicing spelling patterns, memorizing high-frequency words, generalizing spelling patterns, and adding to knowledge and curiosity of unique and interesting words.

Among this plentiful catalogue of word work possibilities, the key word vocabulary process fits comfortably and coherently. A critical feature of D5 organization is the deliberate and sequential instruction about how to get started with the task and how to maintain engagement. A highly valued disposition is *stamina*, the ability of each student to self-motivate during any D5 cycle so that refocusing and on-task attention is consistently achieved.

The steps are constructed overtly and explicitly for any Word Work activity that might be part of the morning's menu. Anchor charts are displayed that help students remember the sequence to carrying out a given task.[5] In a D5 structure, an anchor chart might map the following steps when key word work makes up the Word Study choice for any given day's literacy block:

- Get your key word box from the key word box shelf.
- Find a spot at the key words table.
- Read through your key ring of words to yourself.
- Read some of your words to a classmate.
- Think about what your next word will be.

Word Study with a key vocabulary aspect necessarily assumes a hybrid nature with regard to literacy independence. Keeping in mind that all D5 work advances a drive toward self-reliant engagement in literacy, important phases of the key word experience demand and revere the interaction between student and teacher. Nevertheless, there are countless ways that students can be productive at the key word table as a Word Study/Work choice outside of that special communicative moment when child and teacher land upon a new word to be added to the ring.

The following is a starter list of valuable learning tasks from the key word ring and box program meant to be accomplished independently:

- Use manuscript paper to practice D'Nealian or Zaner-Bloser block letter print writing of self-selected words from the ring.
- Search for and record instances of phonics lessons or rules that reinforce prior learning. Examples might include silent e, digraphs such as *ph*, blends such as *gr, bl*, and diphthongs such as *ou* or *ai*.
- Make sentences using selected key words (a bridge to later writing phases known as *Movements*).
- Discover letter substitutions that form new words. For example, *cat* yields many word family permutations.
- Transfer selected words into spelling practice form using wiki sticks, play doh, or other malleable material.

The watchful eye of the teacher captures appropriate and relevant moments to be stationed at the key word table in order to transact the business of helping students to get new words. On any given day, a teacher might set up for an entire cycle at a key word station. There are many variables that influence how teachers define their time and role during D5 work. Often, they are engaged in reading or writing conferences with individual children.

A cherished principle among D5 teachers is to give students space. The Sisters call this intentional self-extraction *staying out of the way*, which requires a real revisiting of the stereotypical picture of what it is that a teacher must do. This deliberate stance is practiced only during the time that children are selecting their D5 choices. Once everyone is settled, the teacher focuses on the assessment, conferencing, and instructional behaviors that are the foundations of teaching within D5 format.

Management systems, assessment procedures, time of year, and personal style all have influence on how teachers distribute time and attention. But in every D5 classroom, there is the opportunity for a robust, rigorous, and maximal key vocabulary program to be a prime feature.

GATEWAYS TO WRITING

The key word is an emblem of something significant to the child. While any word sits as a jumble of hieroglyphics on the paper called letters, these key words conjure up imagery and emotion that spring from the child's inner world.

Boushey and Moser are opaque and unmistakable about the integral interdependence of reading and writing:

> Intensive work (and play) in writing and word study also supports reading development . . . We have seen a direct correlation between student motivation, ability, and productivity and this increase in writing practice. It goes back to purpose. Kids who have purpose care about their writing and the people who will read it.[6]

The D5 approach includes and highly values a *writer's workshop* format as a fundamental pillar in writing instruction and development. This venerated model of the expressive and compositional side of literacy is seen as a distinct and separate block of time from that which goes on during D5.

In other words, there are two periods of time during the day where children get the opportunity to write. It is during D5 Work on Writing that students especially have the opportunity to work on pieces of their own choice. Mini-lessons that are associated with this writing option in the D5 framework usually have to do with developing spelling strategies.

One of the biggest hurdles for emergent writers is to find independent ways of writing words not yet cemented into their sight word schema. Euphemisms such as *best guess* or *invented spelling* come into play here, all with the purpose of facilitating the drive to keep on writing. Spelling anxiety is suppressed through the encouragement of creativity.

FROM WORD TO STORY

The line between reception of a new key word and an elaborative phrase or sentence (about that very same word) is equivocal. Often a follow-up tidbit of information bursts from the child unsolicited and even unexpectedly.

Take the word *baby*. Given that babies are a popular theme in early childhood classrooms and among pre- through primary-age children, it is not unusual to find *baby* as a card on the key rings of some children. That's the word Israel wanted during a key word session in his kindergarten class. Having traced the word, he took in the work he had done, and announced, "My mom is going to have a baby."

Israel's teacher smiled broadly at this news. Key words can be the vehicle by which teachers learn important happenings in families. She proposed that Israel might choose Work on Writing at the next D5 rotation in order to start a journal entry with just those words: *My mom is going to have a baby*. Israel's acknowledgment of this suggestion included another follow-up assertion: "I hope it's a boy." Israel was set for a productive choice of Work on Writing fortified with stamina, ideas, and a sense of urgency.

The key word process is a launch pad for extensive writing. There is a story in every word. Vygotsky's description runs true that a key word is like a *short tale . . . indeed a small work of art*. Moving children through the leap of one-word captions to the activity of recording the follow-up phrase is the natural and coherent instructional trajectory. Beyond a phrase or burst of a sentence, there is a full-fledged narrative, a tale to be told.

This progression fits well into the writing curricula of many ECE classrooms. From a key word and *doing words* standpoint, moving children through these stages conjures up the musical imagery of movements in a symphony. The term *Movement* is a favorite for describing children's progress in becoming accomplished writers. Chapter 6 takes up movement work and includes several examples of student writing that evolved from their initial key word vocabulary and are samples of student writing representative of each of the Movements, especially II–IV.

DIFFERENTIATION

A reasonable question likely to be posed by a teacher not oriented to the D5 approach is the following: when does the instruction happen? When are children taught how to do the things they are supposed to do independently when they go to one of the five stations? The D5 structure also includes whole group lesson-planned instruction, in the form of mini-lessons between the cycles (or *rounds*) of choice making that students are involved with.

For example, it may be that during the first round, some children are at *read to self*, others have teamed up with partners for *read to someone*, many are invested in *work on writing*, and a few have chosen to do *word work*. The session has gone on for twenty minutes of sustained, attentive, on-task work. The subjective barometer gauge that teachers sport in their internal clock mechanism sends a signal[7] that it is time for a change of pace and a call back to the whole group cluster area.

This *back to the carpet* callback happens two or three times during a typical D5 segment. When children have returned to the meeting spot, a number of events might occur. Most likely, there is some group evaluation of how the previous round went. What was the class assessment especially regarding stamina, sense of urgency, and independence?

There will also be choice making for the next round. And, here is the moment where the teacher or teaching team asks the class as a whole to focus on a particular skill or strategy that would be of benefit to everybody. This is the time for a mini-lesson, perhaps of five or ten minutes' duration, some large group instruction that can be filed in students' memory banks as one other form of input as they practice the stuff or reading and writing. Then, another *launch* ensues as students disperse to their chosen spots for chosen D5 tasks.

The mini-lesson has ended and students are transitioning into their next choice task. What then is the teacher's modus operandi? In order to apprehend the way D5 teachers go about their instructional agenda, it is helpful to consider core components of the daily *CAFÉ* at the root of D5 literacy curriculum.

The D5 *CAFÉ* is the assessment and instruction system that encases the independent work that students are doing as they are immersed in any of the five choices. *CAFÉ* is an acronym that stands for *Comprehension, Accuracy, Fluency, and Extended Vocabulary*. These are the four components of literacy that make up the goals and objectives of each student's engagement with text and material at each of the D5 tasks. Whether reading to self, or mastering a Word Work worksheet, reading to someone or adding to a piece of writing, it is in one of these broad *CAFÉ* skill headings that students focus. How a student has advanced, achieved, or made tangible progress in the given skill is at the heart of D5's authentic assessment.

How does a student come to know the quite particular skill within the CAFÉ headings that stands as the primary objective? This information emerges out of the individual dialogues that the teacher has with each student several times a week. It is one of the major outcomes of the conferences that ensue in both reading and writing and which set in motion the dynamics of assessment and instruction.

Because each student is working on different skills, at different paces, and with the uses of individually selected strategies, the pedagogy at work is highly differentiated. Boushey and Moser encapsulated the broad brush of CAFÉ organization as an enterprise in "diagnosing students' strengths and needs as readers and designing a path of instruction and practice."[8] Such diagnosis forms the basis of charting an instructional design.

> It was this initial learning that shaped our belief that each student deserves a plan tailored to his or her needs. Call it an intervention or one-to-one conferencing or small-group work, to us the goal is always the same: we are meeting each student's needs with tailored instruction.[9]

Table 4.1 is a reprint of The Literacy CAFÉ menu. Under each of the four component areas are lists of strategies that are applicable to the goal of improvement in each of the areas. For example, in support of *Comprehension*, a student might *use prior knowledge to connect with the text*. Vocabulary is extended when a student *tunes into interesting words*. Teachers plan mini-lessons in order initially to introduce students to these strategies. Thus, an exposure to them is formed. It is, however, at the point of conferring, in

Table 4.1 The Café Menu

Comprehension	Accuracy	Fluency	Expand Vocabulary
I understand what I read	I can read the words	I can read accurately, with expression, and understand what I read	I know, find, and use interesting words
Strategies	*Strategies*	*Strategies*	*Strategies*
• Check for understanding • Back up and reread • Monitor and fix up • Retell the story • Use prior knowledge to connect with text • Make a picture or mental image • Ask questions throughout the reading process • Predict what will happen, use text to confirm infer and support with evidence • Use text features (titles, headings, captions, graphic features) • Summarize text; include sequence of main events • Use main idea and supporting details to determine importance • Determine and analyze author's purpose and support with text • Recognize literary elements (genre, plot, character, setting, problem/resolution, theme) • Recognize and explain cause-and-effect relationships • Compare and contrast within and between text	• Cross-checking • Do the pictures and/or words look right? • Do they sound right? • Do they make sense? • Use the pictures • Do the words and pictures match? • Use beginning and end sounds • Blend sounds; stretch and reread • Flip the sound • Chunk letters and sounds together • Skip the word, then come back • Trade a word/ guess a word that makes sense	• Voracious reading • Read appropriate-level texts that are a good fit • Reread text • Practice common sight words and high-frequency words • Adjust and apply different reading rates to match text • Use punctuation to enhance phrasing and prosody (end marks, commas, etc.)	• Voracious reading • Tune in to interesting words and use new vocabulary in speaking and writing • Use pictures, illustrations, and diagrams • Use word parts to determine the meaning of words (prefixes, suffixes, origins, abbreviations, etc.) • Use prior knowledge and context to predict and confirm meaning • Ask someone to define the word for you • Use dictionaries, thesauruses, and glossaries as tools

Behaviors That Support Reading
Get started right away. Stay in one place. Work quietly. Read the whole time. Increase stamina. Select and read good-fit books.
The CAFÉ Book: Engaging All Students in Daily Literacy Assessment and Instruction by Gail Boushey and Joan Moser, copyright © 2008, reproduced with permission of Stenhouse Publishers. www.stenhouse.com

one-to-one fashion, that a strategy becomes identified as a personal goal for any given student.

In one fell swoop, these conferring exchanges create the basis for assessment (how is the child doing initially in applying this strategy?), instruction (how can the teacher model, sequence, break down, and make explicit the strategy?), and coaching (how can dialogic exchanges between student and teacher nudge the student toward employment of the strategy?).

Boushey and Moser conclude that they are offering a system that moves from conferring to coaching. The constant variable is the dynamic that happens at the check-in and individual conference point with each person at each of the D5s. Given that such a variable comports an infinite variety of ambiance, characteristics, content, and behaviors, differentiation is the name of the game.

The D5's monument to the CAFÉ and to differentiation comes in the form of a thick and prized portfolio binder with the name *Pensieve*.[10] This binder is in essence a "conferring notebook," and in it are tabs for each student in the class and a section of record-keeping that tracks accomplishments and goals in comprehension, accuracy, fluency, and extended vocabulary. It is very much a shared tool as the student cues in on self-generated assessments and goals along with her teacher. The name Pensieve connotes the reflective and in-depth quality that D5 literacy work conjures up. It is a register that is wonderfully suited to add observational and commentary notes about key vocabulary to all of the other assessment forms contained within.

Although Boushey and Moser state explicitly that teachers need to personalize their pensieves so that they fit individual teaching styles, needs, and priorities, they also offer an official configuration. Within each child's section, there are three documents: the CAFÉ menu (table 4.1), a reading conference form, and a writing conference form. When teachers incorporate key words as part of the D5 routine, a key vocabulary reflection and observation tab becomes a valuable addition.

THE KEY VOCABULARY AND DIFFERENTIATION

The differentiated system as codified in the D5 approach sets the table for the teacher disposition stance required for successful implementation of key vocabulary work inside the ECE classroom. The manner of the key word transaction is dependent on so many variables that it harkens back to "The Sisters" expostulation that children receive *tailored* planning and interaction in alignment with their needs. Figures 4.1, 4.2, and 4.3 show key word cards from three different students, all of whom are doing key words as part of their kindergarten literacy programs.

Osweldi's ring is filled with words in Spanish and in English. The step of tracing over the word has long been forsaken as unnecessary. His copying is

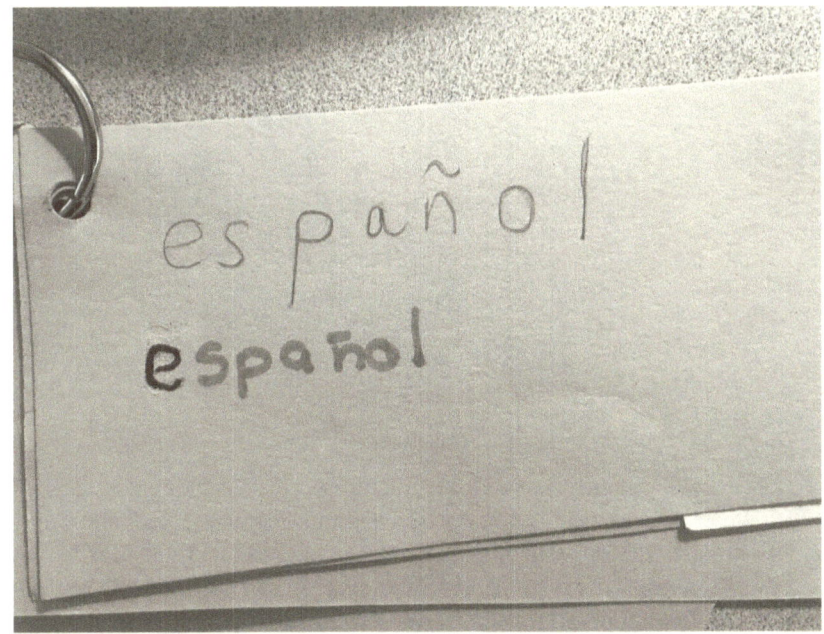

Figure 4.1 Osweldi's key word

Figure 4.2 The teacher's differentiation wheels are turning

Figure 4.3 Aden's key word

precise and calligraphic. Osweldi also demonstrates a developmental stride as his own copied version is compressed and more akin to actual adult printing. His work contrasts with Lexi, who traces over letters (and does so with the out-of-the-box creativity of a different color for each letter), but does no copying. During an entirely different D5 rotation, Aden, who had asked for his teacher's name, *Marletta*, has several sophisticated words on his key word ring, but is in a quite early stage of letter formation. The teacher's differentiation wheels are turning, modifying objectives and expectations on the individual level. Key word work is very much an act of tailoring.

Of course, differentiation has much to do with content as well as skill and learning style. Chapter 3 devoted much attention to the process of identifying new key words for individual children (see *Getting a Word*). Osweldi's example provides much content information. He is proud of words in his home language and his new language. He is so proud in fact that he wanted the very word *español*.

Cesar was a classmate of Osweldi and was just beginning to learn about key words. Cesar's first attempts at the key word table help elucidate the differentiated process of getting words. Cesar started with the very *Mom* first card that is a prevalent first dive into key words. He stumbled after that, having not fully constructed what else could possibly ensue after formalizing *Mom* on a card. Standard questions got posed:

> "What do you love to do?"
> "Play!"
> "What do you love to play?"
> "Tag."

"Who do you love to play tag with?"
"Osweldi."

After *Mom*, Cesar soon had *play, tag,* and *Osweldi* as key word cards dangling from his ring that now claimed four words. Differentiation is often a matter of asking the right question at the right time.

Several other literacy elements come to the fore as the key word process unfolds. Attention to any of these elements is a matter of both assessment and instruction. The teacher is constantly taking in and recording, *Pensieve* style, what a student is able to do in this authentic sphere of reading and writing, and this input drives decisions regarding how to proceed.

These include the following:

- Elements of Print

Especially with novice readers, there is an emphasis in mastering knowledge about what constitutes a letter, a word, a sentence, and even a paragraph. The key word experience is unmatchable for its capacity to enable the construction of the concept of a word.

- The Alphabet

Kindergarten children bring alphabetical prior knowledge to the key word table. In fact, preschoolers are well on their way to knowing ABCs and lots of letters. Early in the school year in a kindergarten class, this familiarity and mastery varies widely. The key word process provides an assessment scope for teachers to observe knowledge in production mode. At the same time, alphabet instruction is supported and fortified as a child names letters contained in these powerful words.

- Phonics and phonemic awareness

The opportunities to focus on sound-symbol relationships within words are vast. For example, Camilla wanted the word *tattoo*. Her teacher appraised a teachable phonemic moment.

"Tattoo. Tattoo. What's the first sound you hear with tattoo?"
Camilla was way ahead of the teacher. "It starts with *T*."
"Yes!" The teacher responded with excitement. "These two letters say *t—a*. And then there's the *t* sound again. *T—a—t*."

The word construction was finished off with an *oo*, said and written with gusto. Ultimately, children are sounding out and best guessing the spelling of their own new words. By that time, they are writing complex sentences, which means they are well ensconced in Movements III and IV (see chapter 6).

- Tracing, Copying, and Direct Writing

Luceta's new word for the day was *cake*. The teacher wrote the word and she traced over it, first with her finger, and then with a pencil. Jessilyn's word was *birdie*. She traced over the word and also copied it below. The copying brought a teacher smile for she wrote it *b ! r d i e*: one *i* sporting a dot on top, the other *i* dotted from below.

When Gregory wrote his friend's name *Jamari*, he used environmental print. He positioned himself near the cubby wall in order to find the labeled name.

- The Writing Pathway

Children are in Movement I as they are acquiring new words and building the key ring to forty or so key words. The transitional moment happens, however, when word clusters take hold as well as phrases and sentences. They have entered the world of Movements II, III, and IV.

With each of these elements, assessment and instructional decisions are paramount. Every decision is tailored to each individual child. Just as the *Pensieve* chronicles previous work, goal setting, observation, and self-reflection in the D5 and CAFÉ system, the key word experience is unique, crafted, and chiseled to the needs of each student.

Of course, the penultimate measure of differentiation comes with the enterprise of assembling a key word ring, dangled with a whole lot of words, chosen by and for the individual student. Imagine an early learning school paradigm where each student totes his or her own key ring—a sign that words are the road to literacy, but each person paves his or her own unique road.

LITERACY LEARNING CENTERS

> Learning centers are spaces within the early childhood setting where materials or equipment are gathered and arranged in order to promote hands-on learning and specific skills, such as large- and small-motor skills, language and literacy skills, creative thinking skills, and math and science problem solving.[11]

> Literacy centers are used during small group instruction to provide application and reinforcement of literacy skills introduced and taught during whole group instruction. Literacy centers allow students to work independently in small groups or individually while the teacher is working with small groups of children with similar needs to reinforce specific literacy skills taught.[12]

Integrating literacy centers into the regular schedule of ECE classrooms is a time-honored and research-endorsed practice. When teachers set up learning centers, they are demonstrating the confluence of child development, literacy independence, classroom management, differentiation, and meaningful, developmentally appropriate practice.

In classrooms that have a long-standing tradition of centers' use, the introduction of a key word choice is a seamless and easily coherent modification. If teachers have not set up centers in the past and are contemplating starting a key word program, such a station format stands as a worthy option for meeting the environmental and management necessities. According to Hodges and McTigue,

> Literacy centers provide a set of individual, developmentally appropriate learning activities that can be updated daily to match current objectives, but do not need to be planned anew. Literacy center templates can be cycled, combined in different ways, and modified for students. Advantages of using literacy centers include differentiation, reteaching, motivation, and technology integration. Using the literacy center framework, the teacher serves as a facilitator who provides differentiated learning opportunities and helps students monitor their own progress.[13]

One of these learning activities can most certainly be a key word table. Learning Centers neither supplant nor reprioritize other literacy instruction that happens in a school day or year; they are complementary to the overall curriculum, but importantly, they are not simply fun-filled extras when there is time or when children have earned something extra. Centers are integral to the whole scheme of reading and writing. Students are doing the work of literacy with a level of independence and choice, as well as a balance of rigor and informality.

The actual look of a center's program varies with lots of room for teacher individuality and personality. A common and universal principle is that no center is simply busy work, or meant only to occupy a student. Every center has a learning purpose. In her book *Literacy Work Stations*, Debbie Diller sums it up by saying,

> Too many times we begin with the "stuff." Many times when I give workshops, teachers ask me to just give them activities. My thinking is just the opposite. I believe if you begin with what you are trying to teach—your purpose, then you can more easily figure out what materials to use.[14]

Diller goes on to paint a picture of what a literacy station's time block looks likes. In a kindergarten or first-grade classroom, there will be a range of five to nine centers (or *stations* as Diller suggests. It is a more descriptive term). These stations include the following:

- Classroom Library station
- Big Book Work station

- Writing Work station
- Drama Work station
- ABC/Word Study Work station
- Poetry Work station
- Computer Work station
- Listening Work station
- Puzzle and Game station

To complete Diller's list, teachers can consider the following: an overhead work station, pocket chart work, creation work, science work,[15] social studies work, handwriting, and the sand and water table.

Each of these centers is introduced over time through a series of mini-lessons that ensure understanding about how to proceed independently. At the point of transition from whole group meeting (or cluster) area to station dispersal, students refer to a visual indicator as their compass assignment. Diller offers as an example a pocket chart with all of the stations mapped, and list of students under each one. Everyone knows where to go, and how to rotate.

According to Stewig and Jett-Simpson, "Learner-centered literacy classrooms are grounded in the principles of developmentally appropriate practice for early childhood . . . and the conditions of learning identified by Cambourne (1988)."[16] Many of these conditions are consistently articulated throughout school discourse and include such characteristics as engagement, expectation, and responsibility, but the condition of *immersion* deserves emphasis when learning centers is the topic. Centers set the table for deep immersion in literate behaviors.

LEARNING CENTERS, CHOICE, AND KEY WORDS

The menu of centers and activities listed above is adaptable to the inclusion of a key word table that serves as a distinct and appealing station. As has been emphasized in previous sections, choice is an integral element in the key word process. Some teachers assign students to particular centers, using a rotation format (as seen in the Diller example above). Another arrangement is to determine the number of slots available at each station. If there is a seat available, a student is free to choose to be at that center. It's a choice model.

In either instance, and with other management systems invented by creative teachers, the option of providing a key word table is straightforward. Within the scope of the Diller model, there can simply be an extra pocket on the pocket chart for people who choose to do key words. What if there are more takers than the table can handle? In this case, the teacher would make an executive decision based on record-keeping notes (a pensieve pure and simple) or goal prioritizing. The empty seat model also works well, no matter what else the structure calls for. When a key wording student has reached a finishing point, the stage is set for rotating a new person into the station flow.

A common arrangement in the literacy centers approach calls for the teacher to use this time for meeting with guided reading groups while the rest of the class is immersed in the various stations. A primary class might have three or four guided reading groups based on a flexible grouping system or an apportionment derived from skill assessment.

The teacher meets with these small groups while others in the class are active in their chosen or assigned centers. When a center's program adds a key word station as one of the activities, the teacher replaces guided reading for a day or even just for a rotation so that she can facilitate the key word steps. The rest of the class is occupied as always, in the variety of enticing centers that have been set up.

It is important to note that in so many ECE classrooms, the lead teacher is not the only educator in the room. As more and classrooms add para-educators, literacy coaches, pull-in special education teachers, preservice interns, and parent volunteers, the possibilities are endless for how the key word station will be staffed. One of the best staffing arrangements is team teaching, situating more than one certified teacher in the classroom. The key word teacher must be trained, know the children well, and have a solid understanding of literacy development, but a school dedicated to the power of key words has in its grasp the opportunity to prepare several staff per classroom to facilitate the process.

KNOWING WHAT AND WHY

Learning centers provoke a manner of thinking and cognition in children that does not necessarily come about during other parts of the day. Students are presented with choices, and decision-making brings with it an opportunity to reflect upon why a particular choice was made. Students are engaged in self-discovery and take an inward look into their decision process. Giving someone the chance to explain why a choice has been made stretches thinking and self-awareness.

A study by Cunningham, Zibulsky, and Callahan[17] demonstrated that children were quite adept at naming each center and describing what was supposed to happen there. Less evident was their ability to say why a certain center was educational or what the purpose was. Nevertheless, this naming expertise is important because it mirrors the cognitive organizational development of children when the structure of their environment is made explicit and learning activities are labeled.

An important attribute of the key vocabulary program is its intentionality; children know that key words are a special activity distinct from other classroom tasks, which elevates its meaning and importance. By the same token, it is important that teachers prompt and assess students' understanding about what key words achieve. When students can explain what and why they are learning, they are exercising their cognitive muscles and achievement increases.[18] This aspect of cognition has itself acquired the term *student voice* and has become a prime focus for teacher planning.

AUTHENTIC ASSESSMENT

The use of literacy centers provides the conditions for authentic assessment as has been defined by a plethora of researchers and theorists. Authentic assessment strives to describe and situate a student's skill level, progress, and mastery as indicated by regular, everyday, and common tasks performed during instructional periods. Distinct from specialized and noncontextualized assessment instrument administration, authentic assessment is observation driven and is conducted mid-stream as students go about their regular business. It is the observational and assessment offshoot of centers' participation and activity. According to Morrow,

> quality assessment should be drawn from real-life writing and reading tasks . . . its essence is assessment activities that represent and reflect the actual learning and instructional activities of the classroom and out-of-school world.[19]

Morrow goes on to list seven objectives for this form of assessment. Of particular note are the following:

- Assessments should be observations of children engaged in authentic classroom reading and writing tasks.
- Assessment should be continuous over a substantial period.
- Assessment should take into account the diversity of students' cultural, language, and special needs.
- Assessment must be knowledge-based and reflect our most current understanding of reading and writing processes.

Although not entirely synonymic, the term *naturalistic* is often used in conjunction with describing the features of authentic assessment.[20] The implication is that a meaningful take on how a student is doing, what skill level has been achieved, what are areas of concentration for future growth, and what knowledge, skills, and dispositions are evident—all of these observational points are highly manifested during the work stations that make up literacy centers. The key word table falls easily into this mix. Documentation of the following items helps create a literacy profile and informs succeeding key word instruction in a pronounced way. For any given student:

- What is the fluency level of reading her own words on the key word ring?
- What are knowledge indicators of features of print: distinctions between letters, words, and sentences?
- How is phonological knowledge evidenced?
- What are patterns for identifying new words?
- What is the stage of new word assimilation: tracing the word with index finger, tracing with crayon or pencil, copying word?
- What is the level of word construction? Does the student make best guess attempts?
- What are indicators of readiness to advance to Movements II, III, and IV?

The assessment processes named above fall under the banner of *formative assessment*. Given that the purpose of assessment is to drive instruction, it has been said that formative assessment is *for* learning and summative assessment is *of* learning.

At the key word table, the teacher is continuously weighing assessment indicators as part of deciding where to go next with an individual student. Although this data fit well into an anecdotal notes format, the use of more formal or standardized records adds additional scope and allows key word progress to align with all of a classroom's language arts protocols.

For example, a common rubric used at the kindergarten level would contain features as exemplified by the Elk Grove Unified School District, which is recreated in table 4.2.[21]

Here is a rubric that charts a student's understanding and response to a prompt. In the case of doing words, the prompt soliciting a new word is generally open-ended given that the objective is to identify a new key word. Among many prompts available are questions as simple as "What will be your next word?" or "What do you like to play?" The intent of the criteria is to assess cognitive adherence to the process. Does the child track what's going on? When applied to key words, this rubric helps paint a simple and succinct picture about whether a child is making sense of what key vocabulary is all about.

The conventions prompt can be utilized directly as students go about copying, or originating their own words. Once a student is launched into the actual writing process, the rubric maintains its relevance and usefulness.

Table 4.2 Informative/Explanatory Text-Based Rubric, Elk Grove Unified School District (EGUSD)—Grade K

	4 Above Grade Level	3 At Grade Level	2 Approaching Grade Level	1 Below Grade Level
Focus/ Opinion CCSS*: ⌐ W—2	• Responds with all statements related to the prompt	• Responds with all statements, phrases, and/or drawing(s) related to the prompt	• Responds with most statements, phrases, and/or drawing(s) related to the prompt	• Responds with some or no statements, phrases, and/or drawing(s) related to the prompt
Organization CCSS: ⌐ W—2	• Identifies topic in introductory sentence • Supplies some facts about the topic • Provides some sense of closure	• Identifies topic about which they are writing • Supplies some information about the topic	• Identifies topic about which they are writing in a student-dictated phrase or sentence • Attempts to supply some information but may be unrelated to topic	• Identifies opinion in drawing(s) or not at all • Supplies no information about topic
Language- Conventions of Grammar and Usage CCSS: ⌐ L—1a	• Prints all upper- and lowercase letters correctly • Demonstrates mastery of proper spacing between all words and word placement on the lines	• Prints many upper- and lowercase letters correctly • Demonstrates proficiency of proper spacing between most words and word placement on the lines	• Prints some upper- and lowercase letters correctly • Demonstrates some proficiency of proper spacing between words and word placement on the lines	• Prints few upper- and lowercase letters correctly • Demonstrates little to no proficiency of proper spacing between words and word placement on the lines

*CCSS—Common Core State Standards alignment ("W" = Writing strand; "L" = Language strand)

WALK TO READ, RESPONSE TO INTERVENTION, AND INTERVENTION PROGRAMS

Walk to Read (WtR) is a structural and scheduling system that codifies ability grouping in reading across grade levels and primary clusters, rather than simply within individual classrooms. Children in kindergarten and first and second grades disperse from their homerooms after opening bell rituals and spread throughout the primary wing of an elementary school, each person headed for his or her assigned leveled reading group. Students meet with their ability team rather than grade-level peers.

WtR is designed to intensify reading instruction in order to overcome achievement gaps. The WtR time block typically hovers around ninety minutes. This time span can be a challenge to developmentally appropriate principles about concentration, brain fatigue, and the kinesthetic demands of five-, six-, and seven-year-olds. Thus, a variety of activities and frequent *brain breaks* are a necessity. A balance of large group, small group, and individual instruction as well as practice activities is a requirement.

A WtR schedule might read as follows:

(30 minutes) Large Group Instruction
(15 minutes) Partner Task (based on just completed skill instruction)
(30 minutes) Small Group Guided Reading
(10 minutes) Individual, tier 3 skill focus
(5 minutes) Closure

The content of the whole group meeting emphasizes *Teacher Read Aloud, High Frequency and Phonics/Structural Analysis activities, Comprehension Strategies*. The small group meets for lessons on *Phonics, Word Work, and Fluency Practice*.[22]

Research about WtR outcomes is variable and indeterminate. *Reading First* has issued a manifesto of established principles that undergird a school's decision to adopt a WtR style of doing literacy. These standards include the following:

- Interventions must provide the opportunity for explicit (direct) and systematic instruction and practice.
- Interventions must include cumulative review to ensure mastery.
- Interventions must provide skillful instruction including good error correction procedures, along with many opportunities for immediate positive feedback and reward.
- Interventions must be motivating, engaging, and supportive—a positive atmosphere is essential.

The last bullet demonstrates the benefit of the inclusion of a key word/key vocabulary segment. The following is an example of how the incorporation of key words into the protocols of a WtR session might play out:

Fifteen primary-grade students convene from various classrooms at Room 2B, which belongs to Ms. Odim. Each student is carrying his or her Read Well workbook, a pencil and crayon plastic case, and his or her key word ring. Ms. Odim greets the children and begins a review, starting with a drill through of sight words.

The read-aloud for the day is *The Big Orange Splot*.[23] During the reading, Ms. Odim asks comprehension questions and comments on illustrations. When she comes to the phrase "all my dreams," she notes out loud to the class that Stephanie has the word "dream" for a key word.

Students are dismissed to three guided reading groups. Two of the groups work independently. In her first rotation, Ms. Odim has the five children get out their word rings. She wonders aloud what words will get added today. Lucera responds, "I want 'house.'" Ms. Odim acknowledges that "house" would be a fine word to add and asks the group if anyone knows how to say house in Spanish. Several of the children simultaneously say "casa."

Ms. Odim directs everyone in the small group to turn to a partner and take turns reading from their rings. She observes and listens in carefully, making anecdotal notes about individual key word fluency as well as strategies used when recall is not automatic. She simultaneously prepares a card with "house" on it for Lucera, and informs the group that she is ready to help each person get a new word.

While she works with each student individually, the others proceed to copy their words on to manuscript paper. This key word segment lasts for ten minutes. Ms. Odim places a straw basket in the middle of the table, and the group drops their rings in it for safekeeping until the rotation is over. The remaining guided small group time is spent with a predictable text reproducible book that is part of the Read Well curriculum.

When a key word segment is added to the agenda of a WtR literacy format, the quality of engagement and motivation is made a high priority. All of the attributes of differentiation are held in place even as generally scripted programs take up the majority of time. The image of a hundred or more children lining up to *walk* to their designated WtR classroom, each clutching a key ring full of words that are special to them and their stories, offers a glimpse of an early childhood community steeped in literacy.

HIGHSCOPE AND KEY WORDS

The HighScope approach to early learning is a widely popular and historically proven set of principles, materials, standards, and curriculum guides that accrue all together into a system of best practices for teaching young children. HighScope is grounded in constructivism learning theory, positing children themselves as prime agents in the development of their knowledge. It has a developmental foundation and is rooted in the theories of Dewey, Piaget, Erikson, Hale, and many others, all with common allegiance to the notion that children actively participate and are engaged in their own learning.

Debra Sullivan, author of *Cultivating the Genius of Black Children*,[24] summarizes the *Active Participatory Learning* philosophy that is at the heart of HighScope's message:

> Children have direct, hands-on experiences with people, objects, events, and ideas. They make choices, follow through on their own plans and decisions, and develop creative problem-solving ideas.[25]

The activities that make up a *doing words* and key word curriculum blend with and are supportive of all that goes on in HighScope classrooms. The original developers of this approach were dedicated to the idea of children having a sense of personal control.

According to HighScope theorists, such control is cultivated throughout the process of active participatory learning. Although active learning is sure to spark immediate images of children who are busy and engaged, the HighScope protocol adds a quite detailed and thorough picture as to what is going on in a participatory environment. There are five ingredients in the active participatory schema. They are *choice, material, manipulation, child language and thought,* and *adult scaffolding.* Each of the ingredients conjures vivid links to the key word enterprise. Table 4.3 maps each of the ingredients, explanatory axioms from HighScope pedagogy, and significant applications in key word work.

The HighScope schedule is designed purposefully to provide as much time as is possible for active participatory learning. Therefore, as in other developmental and constructivist models, most of the instructional time is taken up with children dispersed among the many learning stations and centers that have been set up in the environment. However, there is an iconic systems feature contained within the HighScope approach that renders these programs unique and exemplary. This is the *plan—do—review* practice, the well-known cornerstone of curriculum that sets this model of ECE apart from others.

The thrust of this cognitive exercise routine is to bookend the developmentally appropriate initiative taking that is typical of children four to six years of age with language and reflection that communicates intent (planning) and recall (review). Prior to a transition ritual signaling the beginning of the work time, children are expected to announce or otherwise indicate what activity they will choose.

Table 4.3 Active Participatory Learning Compared to Key Word Activity

Ingredient	HighScope	Key Word Practice
Choice	Pursuit of personal interest Choice of activities Choice of materials	Pursuit of personal images Choice of words for the ring Choice of copying, tracing, illustrations, embellishments
Material	Abundant age-appropriate materials	Cards, hole punch, colored pencils, crayons
Manipulation	Explore, combine, transform	Maintenance of the key word ring and box
Child Language and Thought	Talk about experiences Describe what they are doing Integrate new experiences into existing knowledge	Requesting new words Follow-up conversation about any given word Extended vocabulary: new words attached to experiences and interests
Adult Scaffolding	Support, challenge, provoke Create a zone of proximal development Give-and-take conversational style Teacher maintains a "guide on the side" attitude Respect children's mishaps for their educational value	Co-construction of new words Students are facilitated to copy words, try writing their own words, add a phrase (Movements II and III), and/or write a story about a word (Movements III and IV)

As Wiltshire notes, "In order to plan, children must be able to hold in mind a picture of something that is not actually present or that has not yet happened."[26] In keeping with the Piagetian notion of conservation,[27] the planning process impels children to overlay their active learning with intent and with abstract language. When a child announces, "I am going to build a castle with blocks," she is both asserting an intention of commitment and at the same time explicating the image in her mind of what the yet-to-be-built structure will look like. These are cognitive leaps for young children.

It is a natural modification to add a key word table to the menu of choices at hand in a HighScope environment. Once a key word program has been initiated and ritualized to the degree that children recognize and can name *key words* as a choice, the planning process absorbs this literacy activity as a welcome and suitable option. "I am going to do key words" becomes a pronouncement alongside "I am building with blocks," "I am going to read in the library corner," or "I am going to paint in the art studio." These are the plans as set forth by a community of learners, each individual expressing autonomy and self-possessed intentionality.

This kind of planning runs a trajectory from the general to the detailed and specific. "I am going to build a castle" conveys much more information than "I am going to play with blocks." In the same way, a projection about key word involvement may carry with it a blueprint of the actual literacy that is about to take place. When a child names the next words he is going to get, or expresses the desire to write sentences about a previously hole-punched word, ownership of the key word process deepens even more. The teacher, alert to these declarations, arrives at the co-construction experience of landing upon a new word equipped with this background material.

The *review* (recall) stage of the HighScope template requires a final gathering of the class in order to look back on the work time that just took place. It is evaluative and reflective, and, most importantly, it is a time to finish the cycle of having carried out a previously announced plan. According to Wiltshire,

> There is great personal interest in telling someone about something you have done, and recall time promotes natural speaking, listening and thinking opportunities for children in the company of others.[28]

The review component embedded in the HighScope approach is enriching and advantageous to the process of doing words. It provides an immediate feedback loop for children who have just added to their word collection and creates the condition of immediate reinforcement for what was just learned. Children both affirm that they carried out the aforementioned plan and have a chance to share the new words they have added with the group, not to mention the stories that so often accompany key vocabulary.

The materials-rich environment of HighScope classrooms is consistent with a key word philosophy. It is only within a context where self-guided exploration is encouraged that children have full permission to express the inner life that reveals those special words. At the same time, HighScope theorists recognize that adult-child interactions form the relationship foundations that allow a child to be fully present.

Teachers are trained to engage in back-and-forth talk with individual children and with group clusters, consistently plowing for children's intentions and reflections about what they are discovering with the materials. In the free flow of busy work time, immersed in an environment filled with art supplies; natural world artifacts; supplies that promote cognitive growth in math, science, and language arts; musical paraphernalia; an abundance of children's literature; and stuff to inspire play of all sorts, key vocabularies are waiting to burst forth.

CONCLUSION

Incorporating a key word and *doing words* program into the fabric of an early learning curriculum and daily schedule can be exciting while also a bit daunting. The classic texts that lay out the key vocabulary scheme (*Teacher, Spinster, Doing Words*) paint a system that places the input and output phases of the work at the center of curriculum.

Literacy as well as other content areas are built around the core logic of percolating up the captions of the internal imagery of every child. The creative activities that make up this percolation environment are very much the same as can be found in all developmentally appropriate and best practices programs: paint, molding material, clay, carpentry, blocks, dramatic play, investigatory objects, manipulatives, and so on.

A key word program, however, need not uproot the extant program and schedule in any classroom that has been carefully crafted taking into account state standards, developmental guidelines, and historically acclaimed approaches to early learning. Key word work can fit into classroom structures in ways that not only circumvent disruption and complication; rather, this activity produces harmony by complementing, enriching, and paying tribute to these research-based designs.

This chapter maps such integration with regard to four popular and proven approaches: the D5, Literacy Centers, WtR, and HighScope. There are many other organizational ways of doing literacy that respect child development and show allegiance to emergent literacy. A key word program is adaptable to all of them, as it revolves around the commonest of common cores: namely that children are driven toward literacy just as surely as they are driven toward growing bigger, getting stronger, and becoming more adept at being in the world.

NOTES

1. *Spearpoint* does include stories about Ashton-Warner's negotiations with reluctant students. However, in every instance trust and motivation are achieved.
2. Gail Boushey and Joan Moser, *The Daily 5: Fostering Literacy Independence in the Elementary Grades* (Portland, ME: Stenhouse, 2006).
3. Sylvia Ashton-Warner, *Spearpoint: Teacher in America (*New York: Vintage, 1972), 81.
4. Boushey and Moser, *The Daily 5*, 85.
5. Anchor charts are vivid posters displayed in easy and plain sight for student reference. They list reminders and directions for given tasks.
6. Bouchey and Moser, *The Daily 5*, 80.

7. An uncommon feature of the Daily 5 structure is that buzzers and bells do not determine transitions beyond a standard time schedule for the beginning and end of the block. Within the time frame, teachers are dependent on gauging how it is going day by day. There might be two rounds or three or even four on any given day. Intuition determines that it is time to call the class back to the carpet.

8. Gail Boushey and Joan Moser, *The CAFE Book: Engaging All Students in Daily Literacy Assessment & Instruction* (Portland, ME: Stenhouse, 2015), 10.

9. Bouchey and Moser, *The CAFÉ Book*, 10.

10. As "The Sisters" explain, the term *Pensieve* comes from the Harry Potter series. Dumbledore stored his important thoughts in a vessel called a Pensieve.

11. Evelyn Petersen, *A Practical Guide to Early Childhood Curriculum: Linking Thematic, Emergent, and Skill-based Planning to Children's Outcomes*, 2nd ed. (Boston, MA: Allyn & Bacon. 2003), 30.

12. Rachel Long and Debora Harris, "Using Literacy Centers to Differentiate Instruction in the Kindergarten Classroom." Workshop presented at the Annual Conference of the National Association for the Education of Young Children, 2008. Dallas, TX: NAEYC.

13. Tracey Hodges and Erin McTigue, "Renovating Literacy Centers for Middle Grades: Differentiating, Reteaching, and Motivating," *Clearing House: A Journal of Educational Strategies, Issues and Ideas* 87, no. 4 (2014): 155–60.

14. Debbie Diller, *Literacy Work Stations: Making Centers Work* (Portland, ME: Stenhouse, 2003), 9.

15. Beth Van Meeteren and Lawrence Escalada, "Science and Literacy Centers: This Win-win Combination Enhances Skills in Both Areas," *Science and Children* 47, no. 7 (2010): 74–78.
Meeteran and Escalada offer the hypothesis that engagement in a science center such as inclines and ramps will generate vocabulary and that is intellectually stretching. Words such as ricochet or angle can become prime key words on someone's ring.

16. John Stewig and Mary Jett-Simpson, *Language Arts in the Early Childhood Classroom* (Belmont, CA: Wadsworth, 1995), 223.

17. Anne Cunningham, Jamie Zibulsky, and Mia Callahan, "Starting Small: Building Preschool Teacher Knowledge that Supports Early Literacy Development," *Reading and Writing* 22 (2009): 487.

18. Athanasia Chatzipanteli, Vasilis Grammatikopoulos, and Athanasios Gregoriadis, "Development and Evaluation of Metacognition in Early Childhood Education," *Early Child Development and Care* 184, no. 8 (2014): 1223–32.

19. Lesley Morrow, *Literacy Development in the Early Years: Helping Children Read and Write* (Boston, MA: Pearson, 2012), 43.

20. Jennifer Grisham-Brown, Rena Hallam, and Robyn Brookshire, "Using Authentic Assessment to Evidence Children's Progress toward Early Learning Standards," *Early Childhood Education Journal* 34, no. 1 (2006): 45–51.

21. EGUSD—Informative/Explanatory Text-Based Rubric, Grade K (blogs.egusd.net/ccss/files/2013/10/K.Informative.Rubric).

22. National Center for Reading First, http://www2.ed.gov/programs/readingfirst/support/principal.pdf.

23. Daniel Pinkwater, *The Big Orange Splot* (New York: Turtleback, 1993).

24. Debra Sullivan, *Cultivating the Genius of Black Children: Strategies to Close the Achievement Gap in the Early Years* (St. Paul, MN: Redleaf Press, 2016).

25. Sullivan, *Cultivating the Genius of Black Children*, 15.

26. Monica Wiltshire, *Understanding the HighScope Approach: Early Years Education in Practice* (New York: Routledge, 2012), 68.

27. In Piaget's theory of conservation, the child realizes that properties of objects—such as mass, volume, and number—remain the same, despite changes in the form of the objects (https://www.sciencebuddies.org/science-fairprojects/project_ideas/HumBeh_p049.shtml#background).

28. Wiltshire, *Understanding the HighScope Approach*, 68.

Chapter 5

Cultural Excavation

A key word approach unlocks a treasure chest of cultural context for each and every child. As such, the rationale behind seriously considering the infusion of key words into ECE pedagogy goes beyond the merits of pure literacy efficacy and reaches the sublime realms of relevancy, meaning, and identity. Elementary and especially primary classrooms in the four corners of the nation, urban and rural, monolingual and bilingual, with and without school improvement mandates, are universally grappling with what it means to be culturally relevant. How does a teacher create learning environments that honor culture, recognize culture, make room for culture, and view each child as a cultural person? How do kindergarten and first-grade teachers demonstrate that food, fairs, folktales, and festivals[1] are not the hallmarks of cultural competence, and that true understandings about equity literacy and cultural relevance are prerequisites for equitable learning environments?

Key word pedagogy powerfully contributes to an authentic and meaningful system for respectful inclusion of a cultural and multicultural dimension. There are five distinct, while also intertwined, principles that summon up how the best practices of cultural responsiveness integrate naturally with a key vocabulary program:

- Know each child well.
- Practice diversity pedagogy.
- Centralize family as the anchor and meaning-making point for the child.
- Exploit linguistic diversity for all of its educational potential.
- Search for ways to develop critical consciousness about what is fair and what needs to be changed.

KNOW EACH CHILD WELL

The professional development decree that teachers must really know the child has unabashedly achieved canon distinction as a classroom imperative. According to the Developmentally Appropriate Practices manifesto produced by the National Association for the Education of Young Children (NAEYC),

> Teachers make it a priority to know each child well, and also the people most significant in the child's life. Teachers establish positive, personal relationships with each child and with each child's family to better understand that child's individual needs, interests, and abilities.[2]

It is literally impossible to carry out a successful teaching and learning program without insight into the learning styles, the strengths, the challenges, the interests, the histories, and the stories that each student comports daily into the fabric of a learning community. Every one of the attributes listed above manifests links to deep cultural values and meaning making.

A cultural volcano metaphor is often employed as a signification of the deeply rooted (though sometimes unaware) influence that cultural forces have on an individual's makeup. For example, the interpersonal ability that is named as one of eight in the multiple intelligences scheme postulated by Howard Gardner[3] is affiliated with cultural ways of being that are dependent on communalism and the value of group cohesion. Key word work is uniquely positioned to take advantage of interpersonal affinity because children are situated in a cluster fashion with lots of interactivity as they mutually delve into their own specialized words. It is a preeminent example of the uncommon shared commonly.

Teachers are compelled to know the intelligence profile of individual children: verbal/linguistic, kinesthetic, musical, logical/mathematical, and so forth. The key word experience reveals much about a child's way of being intellectually. By the same token, a teacher's knowledge of each child will have a potent influence in how key words sessions are structured and move along.

KNOW WHAT INTERESTS THE CHILD

Perhaps the most vivid manner in which key word enterprise answers the call to know each student well is manifested in the content material that is rendered in word identification and elaboration. When, for example, Saulo asked for *horse* as his next word, the teacher gained an immediate scope into his relationship with animals.

In fact, the key word card with *horse* on it turned into a dual-language exercise because Saulo requested *caballo* to be written on the other side. Having traced both words and imprinted a fine illustrated rendition of an equine figure, Saulo proceeded to announce to the teacher, "I have a caballo in Mexico." Here is information the teacher did not know before and is rich in instructional potency. Not to mention, when a child in class possesses a horse, the teacher ought to know about it.

The concept of *transnationalism*[4] has gained much enfranchisement in schools and classrooms that serve immigrant populations of any generation. One of the inspiring and hopeful developments in schools' pursuit of thoughtful approaches to so much ethnic, cultural, and national diversity of family makeup is to value such heritage and background as strengths to be honored rather than as deficits to be surmounted.

Many bicultural children, fully in step with their American community daily lives, also claim bonds and contemporary relationships with country/communities of origin. When the stories accompanying those bonds fail to find a listening ear within the structure and logic of the school day, a critical piece of any child's life is shut out and denied. On the other hand, when feedback loops suggest interest, curiosity, and validation, floodgates can be opened.

After Saulo told of his horse in Mexico, ears at the key word table perked up. Classmates discerned that such stories were not only welcomed, they also contributed valuable funds of knowledge to the class community. Veronica's word for the day became *frog*, not the word she had originally intended as she approached key words for the day.

"In Mexico I put a frog in my hand," she narrated as a vivid and warm memory.

Teachers cannot assume that children feel permission for such a memory to make its way into the classroom. The key word enterprise is a permission-granting mechanism.

PRACTICE DIVERSITY PEDAGOGY

One of the most compelling treatises about cultural competence and sensitivity inside classroom dynamics was authored by Rosa Hernandez Sheets entitled *Diversity Pedagogy*.[5] In this volume, Sheets puts forth a theory that an unavoidable dialectic exists within the walls of a classroom in which student expression and teacher response code each other toward either self-revelation or self-shutdown with regard to cultural material.

> This ideology views the relationship between culture and cognition as essential to understanding the teaching-learning process. It focuses on the ways teachers' and students' behavior influences the co-construction of new knowledge.[6]

Teachers are constantly exhibiting what Sheets calls *pedagogical behaviors* with regard to diversity, identity, social interaction, inclusivity, and so forth.[7] Each and every behavior action opens or shuts doors to children's cultural displays. Cultural displays winnow themselves into categories that correspond to the aforementioned areas of teacher behaviors. For example, when a teacher implements an intentional consideration of ethnic identity, students might respond by sharing their ethnic selves more comfortably and in a trusting way.

As an example of this dynamic, Sheets tells the kindergarten story of Tanika during a pumpkin art project. Although the set of materials was similar for all children, Tanika was the only one who fashioned a braided coif for her construction paper pumpkin's hair. And then she announced that her artifact was "brown like me"—an observation that sparked skin color identity conversations in a culturally safe classroom environment. Sheets argues that the teacher is constantly faced with *recognition* or *indifference* as a response to such displays. The direction a teacher takes will have powerful impact on the next dialectical turn of student cultural display.

> The teacher was consciously aware that this was an opportunity to promote development of her racial and ethnic identity.[8]

Sheets counsels teachers to practice diversity pedagogy by

> acknowledg(ing) your responsibility to provide cultural, emotional, and cognitive conditions in classrooms where students from different ethnic, linguistic, and cultural groups feel safe to learn what is intended.[9]

Student cultural display is a natural auxiliary to the naming and possessing of a key word ring set. For any child, the very act of identifying what is important, what she likes to play, whom does she love, what is special—these are all questions that resound in culture and social as well as personal identity.

An example of cultural display is six-year-old Ariana's arrival at the key word table for the first time. She went through the common experience of figuring out what it was all about. A simple explanation coupled with her observational powers resulted in a joint decision that her first word would be *Mom*. That's all it took for Ariana to get into the swing of things and join the ranks of invested key vocabulary producers. In other words, she was ready for her next word.

"I know!" exclaimed Ariana. "Sister!"

Upon which the attentive teacher inquired,

"Do you want me to write *sister*, or your sister's name?"

"Hermana Nycette!" she responded with emphasis, as if to say how could the teacher not know this was what to write. Ariana's family thus and quickly became a part of the learning environment in a way that was categorically different from a one-shot, "who's in your family?"-type lesson.

CENTRALIZING FAMILIES

One of the most robust expostulations of cultural competence as an ideal to strive for in ECE settings is the *Quality Benchmark for Cultural Competence Project* initiative undertaken by the National Association for the Education of Young Children (NAEYC).[10] This work in progress established as a goal to vault past the tourist notions of holiday observance and food sharing in order to reach a common understanding of the deep meanings of culture.

The work of the consortium that produced the *Benchmark* report resulted in the designation of eight concepts that serve as foundational principles for constructing a set of cultural competence guidelines. The first three concepts read as follows: Concept 1: "Children are nested in families." Concept 2: "Identify shared goals among families and staff." Concept 3: "Authentically incorporate cultural traditions and history in the classroom."

CHILDREN ARE NESTED IN FAMILIES

NAEYC's intention was to provide language that reminds teachers daily that the children who show up in their classrooms first and foremost gain identity, composure, and a sense of self from the family circle of which they are part. Children are nested in families. Among other things, this tenet serves to impel teachers toward deliberative and intentional *pedagogical behaviors* that make space so that knowledge of and stories about families can be central in classroom discourse. It is no small phenomenon, therefore, that family members are reliably some of the first cards children produce as they launch into a key vocabulary ring full of key words.

Both Sylvia Ashton-Warner and Katie Johnson found themselves at various times chronicling lists of words their charges had produced as organic reading had taken hold. As part of such cataloguing in her most famous book, *Teacher*, Ashton-Warner listed the following Maori children and their word stacks:

Moreen: *Mummy, Daddy, Tape [dog], lambie, Kuia, kiss*

Penny: *Daddy, Mummy, house, plan, car*

In her later American setting story (*Spearpoint*), Ashton-Warner actually engaged in a bit of data collection, quantifying the number of times certain words appeared in student writing. Not surprisingly, *I* and *my* were the most frequently used, followed by animals of all sorts, and then *Daddy* and *Mommy*.

Katie Johnson was similarly a reliable record keeper and noted (*Doing Words*) that after one day of kindergarten word doing the following list had been generated, clearly weighted with family and friends:

Blackie, Mommy, Duchess, baby, Wayne, Mommy, Easter, horse, Smiley, Horace, Snoopy, fire, Grampie, Gloria, Mommy, Frances, Darren, Dad, fire, Tiny, zebra, Mom, birthday, WonderWoman, Chieftain, rocket, Mom

Tanya was a six-year-old student in Ms. Quinones' English Language Learner (ELL) class. Her home language is Spanish, and her progress in English acquisition was impressive. She clearly liked to party as was evidenced by some of her key word cards and sentenced strips: *Mom, Diana* (her sister), *My party had a peñata* [sic], *cake, pastel, party, uncle, sister*.

In the same class was Pavendeep, whose parents had been born in India. His ring was literally a roll call of household members: *Ibrahim, Jaabar, Alex, Nazima, airplane, Ramya, Hasina, school*. In the left-upper corner of each card bearing a family member's name, there was a number, 1–6. Children invent different ways of keeping order among their key words (and also demonstrate math skills in unexpected places).

These family names scale to a special place in the classroom, not only because the door is open to the stories they spark, but also because these are words that are read every day. Children live in concentric circles of immediate family, extended family, and wider community—this construct is normalized and ever present. Such familiarity and constant refreshing of the family network can only serve to signal warmth, caring, and respect to parents and significant guardians. It is as if to say the family is well noted, affirmed, and welcome in our class.

By the same token, key word rings are unquestionably game for visits home. A teacher's bemused pride is not to be held back as her five- or six-year-old student confidently and enthusiastically recites the ring for delighted parents. It may well be that new words get added at home, surprises for the teacher to discover when the ring returns to school. A key word approach carries with it all of the good vestiges of the two-way street that ought to be the standard for an exemplary parent engagement dimension in the early grades of public school.

A consistent theme of the parent involvement dimension in early childhood programs is that of elevating parental voice in assessment, setting of goals, and sharing of information. For example, good teachers know that parent conferences are successful when there is dialogue and exchanges of impressions.

When key word rings make their way home and then back to school, parents have opportunities to tell home literacy stories that likely would not transpire without this key vocabulary prompt.

FAMILY ENGAGEMENT IS KEY

The option is always available for teachers to conduct parent education sessions that introduce the key word experience to parents and family members for whom the concepts and theory are unfamiliar. Chapter 7 offers a professional development lesson plan intended for pre- and in-service teachers, but it can easily be adapted to fit the needs of children's family members. Such meetings hold extraordinary potential for the benefits that can be accrued:

- Parents are invited to participate in using the very same creative materials (e.g., clay, tempra paint, play doh, sand, and water) that meet their children every day. As parents discover the thread between this creative process and the generation of key vocabulary, a new appreciation emerges that play material is a tool of literacy as well as being just plain fun to manipulate.
- Parent education around key words helps generate enthusiasm at home as well as at school, thus surrounding students with endorsement of their learning to read.
- As teachers work in a workshop fashion with parents, they get to know family members and build these vital relationships.
- Similarly, parents get to know each other in a relaxed, while also structured, format. The simulation of generating key words will make known important people in different families and family stories that parents and others will enjoy sharing.
- Even as *key words* stands as the topic of a meeting, other parental issues, questions, and concerns will arise. Teachers who are keen listeners of parental chatter have a line and an antenna to the topics parents would like to have addressed.
- Family literacy of all sorts is encouraged and affirmed. Children may find added encouragement to do writing at home. The refrain of *read to your child* can be intoned in this family gathering setting, while at the same time a broad understanding of family literacy is acknowledged. Oral traditions and storytelling fit so well into the fabric of doing words.
- Discussion time can include parents sharing about the interests of their children, and resources (especially children's books) can be identified that are in keeping with what children would like to learn about.

The following is a family engagement story that occurred in a first-grade classroom in the northwest that served a diverse classroom with many bilingual Spanish and English students. It all came about because one of the class members, Ramon, got a new key word: *tamales*.

There is a lot of joking around that happens in this classroom of first graders, with friendly and even goofy teasing that transpires between the kids and the teachers. It was no surprise that *tamales* would eventually become someone's key word because they often appeared and were savored during lunch and snack. During the late fall, as vacation and holiday season approached, one of the teachers could be heard to lament, in teasing tones, "Where are my tamales?" as children unwrapped lunches and snacks.

This tiny bit of feigned teacher mournfulness had unintended consequences. These first graders took the lament quite seriously and several went home insistent that teachers as well as students should have some tamales to eat. Shortly thereafter, the first offering of tamales appeared on the teacher's desk. The student who brought it was a bundle of pride as witnessed by his eyes and his smile. Soon the act of bringing tamales caught on like wildfire, and grandmas, aunts, and uncles joined these children's parents in a regular cook off for the benefit of their students' teachers. Their feeling of pride was just as visible as that of the youngsters.

One day, another kind of gift arrived in this most savory of classrooms. A first-grade girl had not as usual unpacked an extra tamal. Instead, she announced at sharing time that she had written a story about "Tamales and the Teacher," which was set in Disneyland and depicted said teacher in pursuit of his favorite massa snack. The class listened in awe as this student writer read the tale. Needless to say, her pride eclipsed anything experienced so far about this tamales project. The class had literally launched a unit about tamales.

It was at this point that a new read-aloud book showed up in the classroom—the bilingual children's book *Too Many Tamales*.[11] It became a favorite of the class and often went home with individual students for shared reading at home. Meanwhile, home-written tamales narratives poured into class one after another. One story with a science fiction bent found teachers rocketing to outer space searching for the best tamales in the universe. In the teachers' lounge and at staff meetings, it was commented time again that the inspiration for this writing came from home. It was not a school assignment.[12]

FAMILY ENGAGEMENT INCLUDES EXTENDED FAMILY

The story about the first-grade tamales project underscores the point that family members such as grandparents, aunts, uncles, and cousins are very important people. A culturally responsive program looks for ways to connect the whole family to a child's school experience. Extended family names are often part of a student's key word collection. That is a start but can be a trigger for outreach and connection.

The tamales story additionally shines a light on the concept of *funds of knowledge*.[13] Cultural competence demands that teachers become aware of the vast knowledges possessed by families, especially in communities that have been historically marginalized. Equity literacy calls for the school staff to participate in a paradigm shift that critiques the notion of cultural deficits and highlights the actuality of family strengths. So many families of color have been underserved and alienated from a public school system entrenched in one-way communication and a paternalistic manner of interaction. A transformation that communicates tacit respect for families as vital resources for successful curriculum stands as a leap forward in the quest for equity and cultural responsiveness.

The roots of the key vocabulary method, springing from the groundbreaking innovations pioneered by Sylvia Ashton-Warner, originally took hold in classrooms that welcomed parents and families. In these classrooms serving Maori children, there was an open-door policy well before such a paradigm had ever reached the level of educational jargon. Mothers and fathers were present in the classroom all of the time. In fact, the mothers of young Maori children were asked to come on into the classroom to listen to individual students read out loud.

It was the relaxed atmosphere created by the presence of these family members distributed throughout the room, ears attuned to young readers, that merged into an open-door policy. This innovation was truly prescient. There could hardly be a more effective initiative in any kindergarten than to take measures so that each child reads aloud to an adult every day on a one-to-one basis. A student teacher who was assigned to Ashton-Warner's classroom is quoted as follows in the biography entitled *Sylvia!*

> A lot of things have happened since in my own career. I source back to the one term I spent with Sylvia Henderson (Ashton-Warner). She believed in whanau learning—parents, elders, everybody could come in and share. There was never any question in her mind that they were untrained, or non-professionals . . . her method . . . was concerned with the creation of a learning environment, and not just a teaching environment.[14]

Ashton-Warner was welcomed into students' homes well before *home visits* had been identified as a program dimension. She also self-taught herself to become fluent in the Maori language. These are family relationship practices that happened over seventy years ago, and still remain as progressive, for the most part unattained ideals up to the very present.

MAKE THE MOST OF LINGUISTIC DIVERSITY

The presence of dozens of languages inside early grades classrooms has literally transformed the meaning of literacy and the complexion of instructional discourse. There is no dearth of models for literacy instruction among the panoply of multiple languages, nor of the concomitant controversies that parallel linguistic philosophy. Dual-language instruction, bilingual development, English language learning, and second-language immersion are all monikers that ring out loud to educators who have witnessed trends and tackled competing perspectives about language and literacy.

Perhaps the most impactful of all recent scholarship is the emerging evidence that demonstrates cognitive gains and intellectual prowess when children gain proficiency in two or more languages. An explosion of research into brain functionality is investigating whether executive neurological functions such as plasticity and attention span are enhanced by the environmental impact of processing different language systems. According to Conboy,[15]

> Enhanced functioning on nonlinguistic tasks that require executive functions, such as working memory, inhibitory control, and the ability to control attention to relevant versus irrelevant cues, is seen in bilingual individuals as young as preschool and kindergarten age.

There is much science and technical intrigue yet to be worked out in grappling with these questions such as brain development in relationship to multiple language acquisition. It is irrefutable, however, that approaches to and responses about linguistic diversity profoundly factor into an assessment of cultural responsiveness. The hidden curriculum is alive and full-fledged when it comes to whether children's home language is invited, respected, and included in classroom discourse. All of which begs the question: how does a key vocabulary program fit into the pluralistic world of linguistic diversity?

LINGUISTIC METACOGNITION

Language learning is not merely the acquisition of receptive and expressive abilities to function and communicate within a language system. It includes a child's knowledge about languages themselves and self-awareness about his or her positionality and identity as a language user.

Very small children develop an awareness about different languages, and most people have stories about toddlers who just know, for example, when to use Mommy's language, and when to switch in the presence of the linguistically different other parent or significant adult. By the time children matriculate to formal schooling, they can name the language of school discourse and can identify their own bilingualism, as well as ways to say things in other idioms.

Simple language diversity lessons are standard fare for most early childhood classrooms. American children learn to sing songs in Spanish and English, and count in Chinese, French, and often in American Sign Language. As children gain self-knowledge about their own efficacy and place in the linguistic world, this awareness can be thought of as their own language metacognition. They are thinking about their own thinking and learning with regard to language systems.

Eurocentric developmental theory may not have a lot to say about young children's "conceptions about language";[16] however, scholarship is endorsing the self-evident reality that children are navigating their sense of self as speakers of a language or more than one language. In this case, the notion of executive function actually speaks [*sic*] to the selection process that children go through when deciding when to articulate in one language or another.[17] Intentionality and deliberateness are characteristics of such decision-making, and it is logical to speculate that children are keen about the status (power) bestowed upon a language.

Regardless of the broad curricular approach in any school or classroom, this linguistic awareness phenomenon is ever present. Even in ELL classrooms, students (especially those who are bilingual) display a natural engagement in code switching between languages. Thus it is that at any given moment, a new key word request may be accompanied by a desire to see the same word written in the home language.

Osweldi was a five-year-old new kindergartner in Mr. Valdez's ELL class.

His very first announcement upon arrival at the key word station for the first time was "Hablo español!" His first word card contained the word "flores," which he easily read each time he reviewed his increasingly populated ring. This kind of transaction fits easily with the concept of student cultural display as explained by Sheets above.

In keeping with the theory she advanced, the teacher is routinely and repeatedly faced with student home language pronouncements. In question, however, is the pedagogical behavior reaction that messages either recognition or indifference. In this student's classroom, languages were named and explored as a matter of routine. Children and their families were regarded as important expertise resources for vocabulary and idioms.

Van, also a kindergartner in Mr. Valdez's class, anxiously wanted a word card with the name of an important family member. He struggled mightily to retrieve the English word well enough to achieve recognition by the teacher. After some starts and stops, a vocabulary light bulb went on: "Granpapa!" he exclaimed.

Van's eyes were glued to the teacher's pencil as the word *Granpapa* took form on the card. The teacher modeled how to trace the word first with a finger and then with the use of a crayon. Van completed the task and held the card with pride. He knew the next step would be to employ the hole punch in order to add this new card to his ring. Just before he did so, he fielded a question from his teacher.

"How do you say *Granpapa* in Vietnamese?"

Character-oriented logographs such as Japanese, Vietnamese, and Chinese present enormous opportunities for cultural responsiveness within the literacy curriculum. There is hardly a more vivid dimension of literacy in which the teacher, unless biliterate herself, is positioned as a learner along with students in her class. In fact, it might often be that the child in this instance is the more knowledgeable practitioner in the transaction.

Clearly, the goal of such language diversity validation is not to teach home language literacy, or to increase the multilanguage precociousness of monolingual classmates. It is up to dual-language and immersion programs to effect children's second-language acquisition in a meaningful way. The cultural responsiveness priorities that are facilitated by an intentional and equity-based key word system have to do with visibility and validation. The teacher is habitually cogitating about the following question: How can the curriculum be made to go beyond simply posting a sign on the classroom door saying *welcome* in twelve different languages? Using a key word program as a foundational basis, the following strategies can help elevate emergent literacy to a place of authentic practice in linguistic responsiveness:

- Listen for and honor a student's request for a word in the home language. It is important to recognize that such an appeal may not come about as a direct asking. Communication styles vary enormously and the child's wish for *tia*, or *abuela*, or *em trai*[18] may require a teacher's projection or even trial-and-error interaction. An important principle is that students' metacognition will kick into gear as far as distinguishing between words in English and a home language. When a teacher signals the message "You have words in two languages; That's really smart," important steps have been undertaken to disrupt the *disadvantaged* labeling of ELL learners.
- Utilize a *think-aloud* approach when working with bilingual children at the key word table. *Think aloud* is an instructional behavior that promotes cultural responsiveness in general[19] and smoothly fits into the conversational give and take that is the hallmark of key word work. Often a teacher is narrating her own thinking as a way of focusing attention. For example, children might overhear a teacher's out loud self-comment such as "Van's dad is picking him up today. I will ask him how to write brother in Vietnamese." Additionally, *think aloud* presents

opportunities for the teacher to broadcast instances of language diversity for the greater audience. For example, as Tanya read her word card ring at the start of the day's session, her teacher surmised out loud:

"Some of your words are in Spanish, some are in English. Some of the words sound similar in both languages. Some are very different."

Observations of this kind contribute to the normalization of language diversity within a classroom. Key words are read every day. The sound of different languages fills the room daily.

- Take advantage of school to home links and communication mechanisms. So many classrooms have incorporated Dojo technology, which is an ideal mechanism for reaching bilingual parents and families in search of accurate translations for words. Traditional forms including newsletters, phone calls, and face-to-face conversation carry their own attributes for meaningful contact. The funds of knowledge that families can offer are irreplaceable components of curriculum. That families possess knowledge valuable to any classroom is a message infrequently broadcast from school building out to the broader community.
- Draw in literacy connections to multilingual words that have become part of students' key vocabulary. The practice of making connections is sacrosanct in the annals of effective teaching. Both veteran and early-experience (as well as student and preservice) teachers follow a mantra of searching for resources, literature, artifacts, websites, and information that elaborate, extend, or support a student's shared interest or experience. For example, when Rosa was first tracing the words *abuela* and *pajaro* as a couple of her first words, her teacher made it a point to use *What Did Abuela Say?* and *I love Saturdays y domingos*[20] as focus read-alouds during that particular week in kindergarten. Emergent curriculum theory speaks to the expansive tableau of possibility when it comes to thematic content to be excavated by an attuned and responsive teacher.

The practice of connecting such curriculum dots especially emerges as teachers confront the conundrum of holiday celebration. Holidays and their rituals become predictable key words or key word phrases in many classrooms. The specialness of acquiring personal words tends to match up organically with the specialness of celebratory days. As students add holiday words to their card rings, or advance to Movements II, III, and IV where writing expands to sentences and stories, holiday differences can be explored and a window of diversity can be opened. Culturally competent curriculum planning is advanced when students learn about each other's holiday practices, including the fact that some families do not celebrate holidays altogether.

DEVELOP CRITICAL CONSCIOUSNESS

It was on a particularly productive Monday in Ms. Rodrego's class that a group of quite ethnically diverse kindergarteners were clustered around the key word table ready to share their rings and get new words. At this particular session, Manuel's request for the word *icky* had provoked some discussion about the short *i* sound and words that began with this letter. This discussion would qualify as *a bird walk* and a *teachable moment* if such teacherese terminology were to be applied. An impressive list of *i* words was being generated whereupon Luis announced what he would like to have as his new key word: *inspection*.

A puzzled teacher look prompted Luis to say more.

"Don't you know about *inspection*? You know where they make you get out of the car and they do the . . . inspection."

It became apparent that Luis was referring to the ritual he and his family had to go through when they crossed the border from Tijuana into San Ysidro, California. *Inspection* became a word on his ring, replete with all the imagery that accompanied his calling up of the term. As his friends at the table listened in, Luis told more of the story noting that everyone in the family ate soup while they waited for the vehicle and the passengers to pass inspection. *Soup* soon got added to the ring.

A key word program can serve as an antenna to the waves of real-world and sometimes hard world realities that are present in children's lives. Children are actively engaged in trying to make sense of social arrangements that contradict common values of fairness, golden rule ethics, unity, and altruism. The teacher's job is often to excavate children's understandings, questions, and attitude development in order to plan curriculum events that challenge, deepen, provide appropriate information, and scaffold problem solving.

Often the prevailing subtle message in early childhood classrooms about racism, sexism, classism, homophobia, ableism, religious intolerance, and xenophobia is that such topics are taboo—not for the classroom. The confusing and contradictory takeaway for students in the class is that there is something disallowed in voicing questions about race, identity, disability, belief systems, and so forth. Such discourse goes underground or spurts out on the playground at recess.

The key word table is an enfranchising place that allows social identity questions to arise and tender topics to be aired. In one classroom, for example, the word *shelter* was commonly shared by several students who had inquired about homelessness and encampments they had observed. In a different classroom, students greeted Monday and a new week with stories about demonstration marches they had attended along with their families during the previous weekend. In one other classroom, Giovanni expressed much curiosity about the American flag and had added *flag* as a word on his ring.

In short order one of his friends remarked that Canada had a flag as well, and that it looked decidedly different. Here was one more opportunity for a pedagogical behavior response by the well-prepared teacher who in this instance had a book on hand of Native American tribal group flags that were emblems of sovereignty.[21] Seizing upon a naturally occurring conversation about flags that emerged from Giovanni's new *flag* key word, this teacher shared images of tribal flags and the stories behind them.

Teachers are culturally responsive when they behave as detectives who watch for moments to centralize what is commonly marginalized. Children who do not belong to Native American tribes as a rule do not know about tribal sovereignty or about the symbols that create tribal group pride. Even when flags from around the world make their way into early childhood curriculum, it is rare that Indian tribes become part of the lesson.

THE FOUR GOALS OF ANTIBIAS EDUCATION

The examples cited above demonstrate how a key vocabulary program not only is consistent with antibias education,[22] but also can be one portal to maximize opportunities for equity-based dialogues to occur. In early childhood education, antibias education has been promoted on the foundation of four goals. Each is advanced by the practice of honoring children's key vocabulary:

Each child will:

1. *Demonstrate self-awareness, confidence, family pride, and positive social identity.*

    Building a set of key words is an exercise in confidence. An underlying message is that "my words count! My stories are important! I have cards with my family names because they are special."

2. *Express comfort and joy with human diversity, accurate language for human differences, and deep, caring human connections.*

    Every student has a key ring filled with words. They are perhaps mounted on hooks, near personal cubbies, in prideful view. Everybody has a ring, but the words that fill the ring are so very different.

3. *Increasingly recognize unfairness, have language to describe unfairness, and understand that unfairness hurts.*

   For example, a student's new word card for the day is *gay pride,* having just attended the pride parade. At a classroom meeting, this student explains how people continue to struggle to achieve LGBTQ rights.

4. *Have empowerment and the skills to act, with others or alone against prejudice or discriminatory actions.*

   Students discuss that the classroom library does not contain books or stories about LGBTQ families. The class writes a letter to the school librarian requesting suggestions for books to be added.

It is the teacher's responsibility, at any grade level, to make sure that equity, cultural responsiveness, and antibias are ways of life in a classroom. These considerations are built in and extend across all sectors of the curriculum. Approaches to literacy can be obstacles to such responsiveness or can, by their very nature, be allied to the shared goals. Key word work stands resolutely as an ally.

DYNAMICS OF POWER

Genuine cultural responsiveness requires an analysis and appreciation of the power dynamics that shape any classroom. It may seem incongruous to wonder about power inside kindergartens, primary grades, or even pre-kindergarten programs, given a likely assumption that the teacher dictates, albeit benevolently, and children dutifully follow. Yet such a didactic model guarantees that dominant culture values, content, and ways of being will uncritically reign as the norm. Rigid curriculum models are founded upon the assumption that students are consumers of preordained material meant to sustain and maintain educational hegemony.

Such knowledge consumerism is akin to the *banking model* of education, a term coined by Paolo Freire[23] as part of his vast and monumental critique of hegemonic ways of doing education. Coming to an awareness about the imbalances of power that are inherent in an approach that views the institution as the possessor of all that is important is one aspect of another seminal Freirean term: *conscientization.* Terryl Ross wrote in the extraordinary compendium book *Soy Bilingue* that a "personal awakening and call to action"[24] is possible as teachers experience *Aha!* moments about who has control of curriculum, content, and ways of learning, starting with the youngest of children.

A key word approach is posing to each child the question *what are the words that will launch you into reading?* These words evoke the imagery and inner word of children and therefore cannot be preordained. Among such words, there simply have to be ones that inspire children's cultural display. And here is where power comes into play. Well before the reading skills of phonetic decoding, syntactical cueing, or semantic inference have even been introduced, children gain uncanny heights in their ability to read the environment. When they are able to read messages of empowerment, that their words not only count but serve as portals to oceans of knowledge, more and more key words come forth, cultural displays are produced freely, and cultural responsiveness becomes a practice based in authenticity.

NOTES

1. Christine Sleeter and Carl Grant, *Making Choices for Multicultural Education: Five Approaches to Race, Class, and Gender* (New York: Merrill, 1988), 121.
2. Carol Bredekamp, *Developmentally Appropriate Practice* (Washington DC: NAEYC, 2009), 17–18.
3. Howard Gardner, *Multiple Intelligences: New horizons* (New York: Basic Books, 1993).
4. Teresa Huerta and Carmina Brittain, "Effective Practices That Matter for Latino Children," In *Handbook of Latinos and Education: Theory, Research, & Practice*, edited by Enrique G. Murillo (New York: Routledge, 2009), 393.
5. Rosa Hernandez Sheets, *Diversity Pedagogy: Examining the Role of Culture in the Teaching-Learning Process* (New York: Pearson, 2005).
6. Sheets, *Diversity Pedagogy*, 14.
7. Sheets lists eight such behavior categories: diversity, identity, social interaction, culturally safe classroom context, language, inclusivity, instruction, and assessment.
8. Sheets, *Diversity Pedagogy*, 21.
9. Sheets, *Diversity Pedagogy*, 23.
10. Quality Benchmark for Cultural Competence Project. http://www.naeyc.org/files/naeyc/file/policy/state/QBCC_Tool.pdf.
11. Gary Soto, *Too Many Tamales* (New York: G.P. Putnam's Sons, 1993).
12. With appreciation to Sharon Cronin and Will Flores for elements included in this story.
13. Funds of knowledge is one of the most important equity concepts that has taken hold in ECE pedagogy. The widely referenced text is *Funds of Knowledge* by Gozales, Moll, and Amanti.
14. Lynley Hood, *Sylvia!: A Biography of Sylvia-Ashton Warner* (Auckland: Viking, 1989), 118.

15. Barbara Conboy, "Neuroscience Research: How Experience with One or More Languages Affects the Developing Brain." (Commissioned Research Paper by the California Department of Education, 2013).

16. Eurydice Bauer and Beatriz Guerrero, "Young Children's Emerging Identities as Bilingual and Biliterate Students," In *Language, Learning, and Culture in Early Childhood*, edited by Ann Anderson, Jim Anderson, Jan Hare, and Marianne McTavish (New York: Routledge, 2016), 19–49.

17. Ellen Bialystock, "Reshaping the Mind: The Benefits of Bilingualism," *Canadian Journal of Experimental Psychology* 65, no. 4 (2011): 229–35.

18. This is the alliterative word for brother in Vietnamese.

19. Winifred Montgomery, "Creating Culturally Responsive Inclusive Classrooms," *Teaching Exceptional Children* 33, no. 4 (2001): 4–9

20. Karen Valentin, *What Did Abuela Say?* (East Orange, NJ: Marimba, 2010). Alma Flor Ada and Elivia Savadier, *I love Saturdays y domingos* (New York: Aladdin, 2002).

21. Donald Healy, *Native American Flags* (Norman OK: University of Oklahoma Press, 2003).

22. Louise Derman-Sparks and Carol Edwards, *Anti-Bias Education* (Washington, DC: NAEYC, 2014).

23. http://www.freire.org/component/easytagcloud/118-module/conscientization/.

24. Terryl Ross, "Historical Overview of Learning communities," In *Soy Bilingue: Adult Dual Language Model*, edited by Sharon Cronin (Seattle, WA: Center for Linguistic and Cultural Democracy, 2008).

Chapter 6

Movements
Bounding into Writing

Every key word is a caption. Every word is a story. It can even be said that a word is an entire composition. In a famous line from her best seller *Teacher*, Sylvia Ashton-Warner makes the point that for Helen Keller, the word *water*, when first learned, was a book—"a one word book" was her actual phrase.

In the early childhood classroom, therefore, writing is the act of getting down on paper the imagery connected to these caption words. The imagery is not lost or faded; rather, it is elaborated through the expansion of language. It is like a movement in musical terms—the word theme treated with all kinds of development and variation. Ashton-Warner summarizes as follow:

> "All the movements" sounds complicated but they're all the same; they're all one flowing movement, in fact: releasing the native imagery again to use for working material, except that with increasing facility our children now use two words, or three words or four or five, until they can write a page.[1]

Distilling Ashton-Warner's methods, together with the system brought forth by Katie Johnson in *Doing Words*, leads to the discovery that there are six movements. However, in many ways, such a finite number is arbitrary. Movements simply suggest the trajectory of growth and confidence, and knowledge of oneself as a writer. Ashton-Warner was quick to say, "Movements are sheer convenience, interchangeable daily."[2]

With all of these caveats in mind, the construct of Movements is quite helpful in establishing a framework for writing development as an outgrowth of the key word experience. In fact, amassing that first set of key words, whether collected on a ring, in a shoe box, or in a large manila envelope—this is the very first movement in the organic writing symphony. Table 6.1 provides a snapshot of the movements.

Table 6.1 Writing Development Movements

Movement I	• Key word work
	• Building a key word ring with forty words
Movement II	• Two or three word captions (e.g., *hermana Nycette*)
	• First sentences
Movement III	• Sentences as declarations
	• Ritual, repetitive, serial writing (e.g., *I like my sister, I like my friend, I like...*)
Movement IV	• Creative writing
	• Several sentences
	• Elaboration of key word themes
	• Beginning of independent writing
Movement V	• Use of personal dictionary
	• Extensive writing into paragraphs and stories.
	• Use of multiple *getting words* strategies: invented spelling, environmental print
Movement VI	• The writing process, writer's workshop

WRITING AND CONSTRUCTIVISM

To watch a young child become knowledgeable about writing is watching constructivism in action. Rooted in the cognitive and developmental theories of Jean Piaget, constructivism posits a perspective about the learner that accentuates the active, participatory, problem-solving drive that children exhibit. Children are constantly accommodating to the stimuli and challenge of newly introduced skills, while simultaneously making sense of what the skills are about. A child is applying what she already knows (prior knowledge) to new input as it transpires. This problem-solving disposition arrives at an understanding that writing tells a story. To put it more succinctly, writing tells.

The nascent writer first and foremost brings her knowledge to a writing task. Constructivism is based on the precept that children are not empty vessels. Standard developmental research and theory track how children proceed from random marks on paper, to a multifaceted stage of scribbling and ultimately to the infusion of mock letters that appear on paper. The moment arises when an actual alphabet letter (usually the first in the child's name) gets scrawled with a writing instrument. Letters begin to parade on paper. They are meant to say something, but that translation is the domain of one and only one person: the three- or four-year-old author. Emergent literacy has landed.

Throughout the movements of the organic writing process, this constructivism shows its nature. Thus, it was that five-year-old Sofya arrived at the key word table for the first time and got to work. She didn't have a word yet and hadn't put together what key words were all about. She helped herself to a card and pencil and proceeded to write out the alphabet. The letters were a mixture of upper- and lowercase. It was as if she were saying, "Writing, I know about writing. Here I go, I am going to write."

Prior knowledge is a formidable entity when children begin the key word process. As was described in chapter 3, names of family members are a rich source of words. Though the system in purity calls for the teacher to write a name per card, children are sometimes way ahead of that process, listing aunts and uncles as fast as the cards can be snatched from the stack. It is this constructivist paradigm that drives advancement from Movement I to Movement II. Movement II is a breakthrough stage encapsulating the epiphany that words go together—words can be paired up so that writing tells even more. In her novel/documentary *Spinster*, Sylvia Ashton-Warner's teacher protagonist Anna makes a discovery:

> At last I'm beginning to see what these surprising writings are that the bigger ones indulge in during the morning output period. They're captions too. Two-word captions: my shoes. Three-word captions: I want you. And story-length captions.[3]

Also chronicled by Ashton-Warner (specifically in *Spearpoint*), family pets hold a revered place in the hearts of many children. One particular morning, during key word input time in Ms. Quinones's K/1 class, Cesar arrived at the table with a determined request for the word *dog*. Before his teacher even began to form the block letters, he modified the appeal.

"I mean *dog and cat.*"

The opportunity for teacher comment was unmistakable. There are three different words here. They are separated by a space. New writers place an index finger to measure the space. This card could just as easily say *cat and dog*. The word *and*—here is such a useful word; it allows the writer to add more and more things.

Cesar next asked for the word *and* to be a key word. In most cases, *and* does not evoke key imagery as is the criteria for getting a word. In this case, *and* most certainly did, given it was the culmination of such a fine transaction between teacher and student.

Children are learning about the structure of language as they simultaneously learn about important words and the functionality of some common words. In *Look, I Made a Book*, Nina Zaragoza points out an important structural concept called *collocations*.[4] These are word clusters or phrases, most commonly two words that when clumped together are almost meant to be. *Happy Birthday* is one of the examples she provides. Collocations are naturally embedded in the key word process, and in the organic bridge between Movement I and Movement II.

The jump to Movement II is all about the acquisition of literacy forms in order to match the world knowledge that children are gaining. As another example of the family pet nudging the process of early learning along, Michael, age five and a half, wanted the word *hamster*. But then he thought better of it: *baby hamster* was actually the key word card he was after. During the same session he got *fur ball*, which provided his teacher the opportunity to explain how words can go together to make one idea. Katie Johnson (in *Doing Words*) might well categorize this image as Movement I output, and here is a reminder that the movements are "sheer convenience."

MOVEMENT II TO MOVEMENT III

A vivid example of a phrase burst that reflects the elasticity of key vocabulary is Camille's dialogue with her teacher during one particular key word input session:

> "What word will you get? What do you like?" the teacher began the intake of words.
> "Play jump rope," was Camille's unabashed response.

Children are unknowing excavators of complexities about what is a noun, a verb, an action. It is a scope into children's thinking to appreciate how, for some young minds, the action associated with an object is integrally tied up with its very meaning. There is also a cultural-linguistic dimension having to do with the primacy of action as opposed to attribute in defining concepts of objects. *Play jump rope* is a declaration that captures the full meaning of this cord-like item with handles attached.

The enterprise of doing words invariably leads to declarations that are all the stuff of sentences. Here are some samples:

> *I like my room.*
> *My puppy is red.*
> *It is my birthday.*
> *We went to the beach.*

These statements are like factoid announcements and carry all the weight of inner imagery as does a single word. In each case, these writings were treated mechanically just as key words. They were written out on cards, traced, and then copied. And they were read by the writer without the blink of an eye.

These sentence cards can be viewed as the forerunner of the transition to Movement III. Depending on the length of the sentence, they present a useful and teachable moment challenge for a card stock scheme. The card may well not be long enough; in some classrooms, this problem is solved by taping two cards together. Another solution is to employ heavy stock sentence strip paper. These are not merely mechanical applications; the medium is the message. The message is clear: your writing says what you are thinking. You have important thoughts, and they are beginning to require more than just a little bit of writing.

IDEAS

When children arrive at the *aha!* revelation that writing is talk and thinking recorded on paper, they have reached a significant literacy milestone. Developmentally, this insight dovetails with an emergence out of *preoperational* cognition that is filled with magical and egocentric thinking. A hallmark of ascendency from preoperational to concrete operational is the logical thinking associated with constancy: the attributes of some things stay constant even when the form sometimes changes.

The classic Piagetian example is the ball of clay that is flattened into a pancake. Children who conclude that the shape has changed but the amount of clay stays the same are exhibiting this cognition and logic-oriented leap of perceptual understanding. Other names for this phenomenon are *reversibility* and *object permanence*. All of these terms are describing the same process, namely that the child is no longer fooled by the look of things. The eyes no longer rule the brain; in fact, the opposite is true.

One of the phenomena that children come to regard as permanent is the written word. Emergent literacy has as an early objective the realization that a piece of writing always says the same thing. Ideas aren't just written down, but preserved through the process of writing. This is another subtle behind-the-scenes message that is part of the emergent literacy agenda: not only are your words special and important (they are *key*, in fact), so are your ideas. Ideas are the most important and basic bricks of growth in becoming a writer.

Writing curriculum in primary and elementary grades is founded upon several agreed-upon *traits* that are quite universally accepted. Although scheme to scheme there is some variation, the general orthodoxy is to name six traits.[5] They are divided on the one hand as a group of form and style traits and include word choice, sentence fluency, and conventions. On the other side, researchers and educationalists identify content traits. Organization is important. Equally so is voice. But the very first trait is the arsenal from which all the others flow: *Ideas*.

I DON'T KNOW WHAT TO WRITE!

The classic key vocabulary texts offer amusing stories about how teachers treat the situation when a student is devoid of ideas.

> Sometimes he will say candidly, "I don't want to write," and that's just what you get him to write: "I don't want to write." From there you ask "Why?" and here comes an account of some grievance or objection which, after all, just as well as any other idea, delivers his mind of what is on it.[6]

Ashton-Warner was drawing on an experience working with Maori pre-schoolers. Later in her career, she got many a dose of idea resistance with American children.

> "Rocky?" one snowy morning, "Come to me."
> "No, no," shrilly, "Not today. I'm playing with Henry."
> "You'll have nothing to read after recess."
> "I dowanna write today. It's vacation day."
> Carried away poetically with the novel idea, "Vacation Day!"
> at the top of his voice. "Vacation Day! Vacation Day!"
> "We'll write 'Vacation Day.'"
> "I'm going to have Vacation Day. Wow, Vacation Day,"
> which is what I write on his card.[7]

Katie Johnson piped in with her own vignette about five-year-old Jenny who just shrugged in response to "What do you want to write today?"

> "I don't know. I can't think." She slumps, chin in hand.
> "How about that one? *I can't think.*"
> Grin from Jenny. "Okay. Yeah. *I can't think of anything to write today.*"[8]

These examples serve almost as exceptions that prove the rule that, for the most part, children's inner life and singular ideas are coiled and wound, just poised to burst forth. Most of the time ideas gush, and when there is a dam blocking this flow, conversation is the tool that can mine stories. Conversation starters are not necessary, nor are writing prompts. The reason is evident and compelling. The child has a ring with twenty-five, or thirty, or even just fifteen key word cards. Which one is the inspiration for an idea to be written about?

FROM CARD TO PAPER

During the intake time in Ms. Quinones' K/1 classroom, Melissa condensed on a card *I like to play with Monserrat.* This is an example of the key idea extending beyond the one-word caption and spilling over into the world of sentences. But Melissa wasn't finished. *Monserrat is my best friend* was the assertion she simply had to add to the articulation. All of this writing required employing another card and fitting in the entire thought.

Yet more was to come: *forever* was a word squeezed and tagged on at the end. Here was a writer ready to transition to a receptacle more equipped to handle her composition. Paper, a booklet, a stapled journal, a notebook, or a pamphlet? A signpost for Movement III is two, three, or more sentences written on paper and amalgamated in whatever format the teacher is partial to.

FORMULA AND RITUAL

As students vacillate in and around Movement II and III, many experiment and become comfortable with template-like formats that define their writing. Katie Johnson called this stage *the friend formula* and it is an important phase of key word movement progression to recognize and register as part of literacy growth. It is manifested as a list-making process in which the sentence stem remains constant, while a changeable cloze tag is plugged into each line. Bertha had the following to say as she moved away from cards and graduated to a lined theme book:

> *I like to play with Melissa.*
> *I like to play with my brother.*
> *I like to play with Monserrat.*
> *I like to play with Veronica.*
> *I like to play with me.*
> *I like play with Taina.*
> *I like to play with Ms. Quinones.*
> *I like to play with Ms. Argueta.*
> *I like to play.*

This kind of formula output can be viewed as a convergence of key vocabulary fusing with breathtaking competency and productivity as children enter into a stage of industry.[9]

The repetitive patterning that shapes this kind of list making can be a bit disconcerting to adults who have nurtured children through the magic years of early childhood wonder. The work that is happening in this stage is akin to the endless rainbows, hearts, and horse drawings that are mainstays of first-grader artists who only months before were making the most expressive, personal, and creative artifacts. Attainment of representational mastery leads to a drive to practice over and over again the newly learned sketch strokes. Many a parent has lamented the loss of a creative artist as the page fills up with perfected hearts. But older siblings display the fact that creative wonder eventually cycles back.

Whether patterned in a series or isolated as single bursts of announcement, children in Movement III are exercising the power of casting down on paper expository statements that capture the immediate truth of the moment. They are writing sentences that contain the world at that given point in time.

Katie Johnson said that Movement III books read like a series of headlines. The writer has become an information provider who has put syntax, form, and vocabulary together enough to proclaim competency to an imagined audience. The composing of these sentences could be viewed as a convergence of *ideas* and *voice*. The following are examples of these declarations penned by kindergartners and first graders claiming their place in the writer's den:

> *I like Richie. He's my brother.*
> *Ezequiel is my friend.*
> *My sister's name is Ester.*
> *My dad went to California.*
> *My mother's favorite color is purple.*
> *It is my birthday.*
> *I have books about Barbies.*
> *My party had a piñata.*

Any one of these pronouncements is grist for a writing conference. Such conversations hone in on writing conventions and feedback about all sorts of writing objectives. But above all, such dialogue digs deeper and under the headline to find inner layers of the imagery.

In her later years, Sylvia Ashton-Warner was recruited as an adult educator, teaching teachers how to implement the key vocabulary scheme. This phase of her teaching coincided with her American, Israeli, and Canadian years of the late 1960s and 1970s. Prophetic as she was, Ashton-Warner knew her task was to eschew lecturing, but rather to take adult students through the process, as if they were youngsters in a class. Figure 6.1 is a rare photo capturing Ashton-Warner conducting such a workshop.

One of her disciples, Bill Cliett, journaled about this experience as part of his own creative writing:

Finishing the first movement we continued to the second, which consisted of smaller yellow cards with two-word phrases. These two words were drawn from our individual conference discussions. She wrote what seemed to be most important to us at that moment. My first was "golden leaves."

During the next two days we covered the third and fourth movements. In the third we had small blue books, first unlined, later lined, in which we began by writing three-word phrases and ended by writing sentences. The fourth movement

Figure 6.1 Sylvia Ashton-Warner conducting a workshop. Sylvia Ashton-Warner at Aspen Community School Teaching Center, Aspen, Colorado. Ashton Warner, Sylvia :Photographs. Ref: PAColl-2522-7-01-02. Alexander Turnbull Library, Wellington, New Zealand.

saw us in larger green books where we could write stories about anything we wished. When we need a word spelled for our own stories she would write it in the back of our books. That became our personal dictionary. These four movements, in her Maori infant room, would take the children from age five to age seven.[10]

BOOKLETS AND BOOKMAKING

Cliett's warm memories about this professional development intensive unearth another important secret in the *becoming writers* process: the value of accouterments. The progression from smaller yellow cards to small blue books to larger green books not only marks growth and graduation, it also infuses variety and motivational stimuli into the environment. The artifact of a booklet pines for a story to be told and written down. Thus, Movement III is also about a rites of passage undertaking of the demands of a blank booklet in addition to marking the increasingly complex sentences that children are generating.

It would be impossible to list or name all of the different composition paper options that teachers use for their writing programs. Katie Johnson names a *personal notebook*[11] as one of the markers of Movement III. Booklets, stapled books, theme books, and spiral journals all are tangible writers' pads that serve a function of inspiring more extensive sentences. The revelation inside Cliett's testimony is that a small booklet with just a couple of pages makes for a self-contained document, even if only a few sentences appear. It is a book plain and simple, and reflects a completed writing task.

This kind of bookmaking can become elaborate and with some quite substantial results. In some classrooms, even young primary-grade students learn the techniques for creating hardcover bound books with blank pages. Into these volumes usually go the *published* final copy of a written piece that someone has been working on. Such a publication marks the final end stage of the writing process.

Chapter 8 provides templates for two favorite bookmaking projects.

It is the variety provided by these and so many other book constructions that helps keep motivation high for writing in Movement III. Of equal importance is the function of these books to set the table for writing longer stories, extensive journal entries, and creative accounts, all of which portend arrival at Movement IV.

In chapter 3, there is an account of kindergartner Saulo who acquired *horse* as one of his first words. His very next card finds the Spanish word for the same key image: *caballo*. A month and a half later, Saulo was working in a spiral personal notebook. His story is as follows:

> *My Horse*
> I have a hors in Mexico.
> One day I trid to rid the hors.
> I rodem to the prk wen I was a little kit.
> He is a braun horse.
> Un dia, era un nino y yo tra de montaro.
> Lo lleve al parquet.
> Es un caballo café.

Movement IV sees the leap of writing into extended stories that have detail, and the continuation of a narrative. Students have internalized strategies so that they are able to write on their own using invented spelling, environmental print, each other's knowledge, sight word mastery, and of course their own key word ring as a resource. The teacher performs the function of scaffolding this production of writing by reading out loud what is already on paper, asking leading questions, conferring, and coaching. Needless to say, the teacher is also informally assessing the process in order to make judgments about how to construct future mini-lessons and group instruction.

It has been well established that writing is an essential literacy vehicle for young students who are grappling with the exigencies of ELL learning. Contrary to a more didactic pedagogy that teaches decoding and phonics exclusively when students are learning to read in a second language, luminaries in the bilingual development field such as Jim Cummins and Stephen Krashen[12] campaign for the central place that *context* has in the construction of knowledge by any student. Cummins proffers a scheme that advises the following learning tasks sequence:

(A) *context embedded/cognitively undemanding,*
(B) *context embedded/cognitively demanding,*
(C) *context reduced/cognitively undemanding,*
(D) *context reduced/cognitively demanding.*

The learning experiences and demands that make up curriculum for primary-age students working in a new language must be overflowing in content and references drawn from their lives, community, and experiences.

Such schoolwork that is lower on the cognitive demand scale might include conversation and games. The enterprise that children engage in that is most demanding while also deeply embedded in context is *writing*. The best practices pedagogy for all children, and especially bilingual children learning the basics of a second language, is to write. Every day. They need a robust amount of time in the daily schedule to accomplish such writing tasks.

SMALL MOMENTS

Not long ago, writing prompts (perhaps *story starters* rings a bell) tended to be wistfully grandiose or exceedingly general. Many adults remember from their school days being confronted on paper with the question: *what would I do if I found five dollars* (needless to say, inflation would alter the equation if the same theme were used today), or the standard September, back-to-school essay on what you did on your summer vacation. This kind of narrative instruction altogether missed the insight that children are fountains of meaningful experience that registers all kinds of imagery and memories waiting to be tapped.

The understanding that everyday living and experiences provide the richest kind of writing content might well be labeled with a variety of different titles. Lucy Calkins called these experiences *Small Moments*, and in the introduction to her eponymously named book she explained that "what in fact matters most to a child's later literacy are the opportunities children have to take the moments of their lives and spin them into stories."[13]

Calkins describes these stories as *focused vignettes*, suggesting that the everyday and seemingly hum drum happenings of living the life of a five-, six-, or seven-year-old contain episodic material that lead the child into becoming an authentic, motivated writer.

The challenge is to escort kindergartners, new to school, new to formulized learning, and very new to the hieroglyphics of literacy, into the world of printed story telling. Calkins and her colleague Abby Oxenhorn land on the effective use of children's literature as a way of modeling small moment writing and as a provocation to scaffold children's thinking about what authors do in order to bring out the story. The philosophy of the small and focused vignette is to grab hold of the moment (diminutive as it might be) and stretch it out almost like taffy so that the interesting chromosomes (so to speak) that make up the story become revealed. A vivid phrase for this taffy stretching is *zooming in*.[14]

How do children hone in on a moment that might become a story's topic? The menu of strategies is logical and probably familiar:

- Encourage children to connect a chosen piece of children's literature to something about their own lives. These connections are often called *text to self*.
- Tell a teacher's life small moment story that models the elements of the everyday, while at the same time showing how the story can be interesting, entertaining, and attention grabbing.
- Use information about a child that has previously come up in classroom discourse (e.g., a child reported she had just learned how to ride a two-wheel bicycle).
- Once some students are launched into the writing process, solicit volunteer examples from early writers as a way to encourage others in the class.

There is another strategy that blends in a harmonious way with the goals and the principles of small moment writing: for each student, refer to the personalized profile of significant captions that make up the collection of Movements I, II, and III cards and sentences, all of which constitute the key vocabulary. As children add detail and zoom in on the episodes of the caption, they are writing in Movement IV.

Katie Johnson summarizes Movement IV by noting that this writing can begin even with one sentence but can grow into a several-sentence paragraph. It is at this point that students are getting used to the idea that an episodic story maps a sequence of events in an orderly fashion. Johnson relates the story of Matt who was mesmerized by his Movement I key word card *motorcycle*. A couple of days later found a glowering Matt reveal in conversation that a bigger boy had stolen this prized possession. He did get it back though, plus two dollars for gas. Matt had started working with a stapled booklet and the writing was as follows:

I know how to put my motorcycle on the kickstand.
B___ stole my motorcycle.
He gave me $2 for the gas.

From the point of view of small moments, each of these lines is rich for the potential to be flushed out, zoomed in on, and prospected for more detail. A writing conference might scaffold an illustrative explanation about how indeed a motorcycle gets braced onto a kickstand.

Calkins and Oxenhorn provide sample lessons about instructing young kindergarten writers to notice how beginnings, middles, and ends really work.[15] Mini-lessons lead children to think critically about how authors build story arcs. How, for example, does an author bring a story to a close? One of the sublime teaching steps is to model for the students the exercise of touching each page of the booklet as a way of kinesthetically mapping out what event will happen in the prescribed sequence and on what page.

Mini-lessons such as this kind of *touching each page* modeling once again reveal the confluence of children's prior knowledge joining together with the lesson's new information. Nina Zaragoza and Eric Dwyer make the point that children as early as in kindergarten bring with them sensibilities about the way stories work. Zaragoza charted student writing in her own kindergarten and found the surprising quantity of stories that followed sequence as well as cause-and-effect qualities. Noting that cause and effect is "one of the harder styles to master," she shared the following writing sample of one of her five-year-olds:

The Man with the Bleeding Feet by Larry
A man lived so far he had walk a long way. His feet bleeding. He got a napkin with alcohol and wiped the blood off his feet. Then, he felt better.[16]

Children learn the depth of this writing business, and that they are truly capable of becoming these literary storytellers. Having early experiences with the key vocabulary authenticates that it all begins with a precious key word.

All of this writing, from Movement II through Movement IV and beyond, fits into the writing process that is the blueprint for *writer's workshop*. In climate, this workshop format shares much with what has been said about the Daily Five, key vocabulary input time, and literacy centers. Students are all doing writing, but there are a multitude of different tasks being performed because each student is in his or her own writing stage.

The classic writing process consists of the following cycle: brainstorming, drafting, conferencing, editing, redrafting, publishing, and author's chair. As each student drafts, conferences, and edits, she is continually adding to her own personal dictionary of words, correctly spelled, that are frequently needed no matter what the subject. Building and utilizing a personal dictionary is the earmark of Movement V, while at the same time stories grow in length, detail, use of descriptive words, and attention to sentence fluency.

When a student is fully ensconced in the recursive writing process, shepherding a piece from brainstorming to a draft, editing by way of peer feedback, conferencing with the teacher, and self-reflecting about all of the six traits, ultimately publishing by way of a book-making template or use of technology—such a writing process picture, so fully engaged, is the essence of Movement VI.

WHAT ABOUT SPELLING?

The key vocabulary approach offers considerable opportunity for reinforcing and supporting the phonetic and phonemic knowledge that students are working on in formal lessons and as part of their emergent literacy. Key word work provokes instant observation moments for noticing structures of words and sound-symbol relationships. As has been discussed above, students jump to a point at which they are writing their own key words, using invented spelling and environmental print. These efforts make for laudable exercise of phonetic and phonemic knowledge. There is no end to the teachable moments that emerge during the enterprise of doing words.

Sylvia Ashton-Warner viewed children's key vocabularies as working material that could later be used for handwriting, spelling, and phonics. *The Mechanics of Teaching Spelling* is a subsection of the *Creative Teaching* chapter in the most well-known of her books, *Teacher*. Ashton-Warner named a set of words called *general vocabulary*,[17] which today would be called grade-level sight words students are expected to know with automaticity. Children would write these common words along with new key words on the board, to be "easily and cheerfully" quizzed by the teacher.

Perhaps the most apparent phonemic association arises exactly at the moment a child has identified a new word to be added to the ring. The standard question, reverberating around pre-K and kindergarten classrooms everywhere is, "What is the first sound you hear? How does the word start?"

This kind of *onset* focus is the boiler plate interaction and dialogue that bridges alphabet and letter-sound knowledge with actual reading and writing application. Reading teachers know that when a student asks how to spell a word, standard practice calls for enunciating the word slowly and carefully, with emphasis on that very first sound. The student wants *Mom*. *M—o—m*, the teacher stretches it out. Some teachers like to use a slinky devise in order to visualize the stretching. Then the word is articulated again: *Mmmmmm—o—m. What's the first sound you hear?*

The roster of the class is often a literal dictionary of prospects for practicing this phonemic skill of hearing the first sound. At the key word table a student asks for her friend, Sonya's name. *S-o-n-y-a*, says the teacher. *Sssss-o-n-y-*a. *How does Sonya start?* Children's friends and peers become essential early key words for so many in a class. Of course, such lists are susceptible to the naming trends of current generations; nevertheless, learning a friend's initial letter and sound is an organic foray into the world of decoding.

It is worthwhile to say a word about this use of peers' names. Given that key vocabulary work is meant to contribute to the ambiance of democratic classrooms and to the promulgation of classroom community, there needs to be intentionality and conscientiousness about use of other people's names. It is a matter of consideration and respect. A good classroom rule (or agreement) is that a peer must be asked for permission to use his or her name. Such agreement is important when a key word is in question and whenever someone's name comes up during creative writing.

Children learning to read and write in English have the luck of the draw when it comes to those keyest of key words: *Mom* and *Dad*. Besides being the captions of warmth, safety, and nurturance, these words are phonemic gifts of regularity and information. Besides their palindrome quality, they are exemplars of *CVC* word structure. The word *Dad* also opens the door to word families especially as *mad, sad,* and *bad* are likely vocabularies in children's early writing. The parental variants, *Mama* and *Papa*, supply even more phonemic exercise as children listen for a middle sound.

The activity of flushing out word families is a natural outgrowth of generating key words. In Ms. Quinones' classroom, the word *cake* showed up on many different students' key rings. There had been a flurry of birthdays, talk of going to each other's parties, and all style of baked goodies. As students copied *cake* onto cards and illustrated with candles and sparklers, the *cake* family was fully delineated. By ways of complicating the brew, Alondra asked, "What about pastel?" She quickly added this Spanish word to her key vocabulary collection.

Programs that serve bilingual Spanish/English children have the additional phonics advantage of opportunities to point out similarities and differences in spelling and letter use rules about words in both languages. The appropriateness of a key word program for second-language learners was discussed in chapter 5, and this theme is carried forward with regard to phonetic and phonemic knowledge. For example, although the actual produced sound of the letter b varies between English and Spanish, the similarity of occurrence allows for aha! moments. A good example is the word *Barbie* that shows up on the rings of so many children. Though packed with controversy and cautions about social messages this toy conveys, it remains unrivaled in popularity. The word itself is a prime example of the onset sound cropping up again as the first consonant of the second syllable. Phonemics is asking for the novice reader to hear the sound at the beginning *and* the middle of the word. This recognition is a milestone in listening for sounds.

As was mentioned in Chapter 3, another caption with enormous inner-life and internal imagery is the word *baby*. Here is a word that crystallizes an understanding of the key word caption discovery that is the secret of key vocabulary. Even for adults, a meditative taking in of the word *baby* conjures a person's history, biography, and cherished feelings.

At the same time, the phonetic makeup of the word is instructionally ripe and generous—here is another example of the phoneme placed at both the beginning and the middle of the word. This discovery made for much discussion at the key word table in Ms. Quinones' class, resulting in a newsprint chart of words with *b* in the middle. Whereupon six-year-old Osweldi, a native Spanish speaker, pointed out something that had not yet been mentioned, "We say bebe, and b is in the middle too."

CONCLUSION

The child who is engaged in key words almost automatically will move onto more complex, more developed writing behaviors. Conceptualizing this growth as a movement preserves a consistency with the big picture philosophy of key vocabulary. As in music, *Movements* connote a kind of journey through stages of writing. The child's writing fugue blends experience and skill development with ever more sophistication, detail, and creativity.

The movements are flexible and flow into and out of each other. When writing is looked at in this way, it is recursive. A paragraph of narrative in Movement IV might well yield a new key word to be written on a card as in Movement I. In brief summary, Movement I has students receiving new key words, each one on a separate card, to be traced and copied. When two and three word phrases appear, as well as announcement-type sentences, Movement II is in play. Movement III continues this production of sentences. Often, there is some kind of formulistic structure to the sentences. And most importantly, students are introduced to booklets and paper of all kinds. Students are writing.

Movement IV describes students invested in extended writing with the number of sentences increasing even into paragraphs. This is a time of creative writing in which students comfortably use strategies such as invented spelling and environmental print. They write about happenings in their own lives called small moments. Movement V is much like Movement IV with the addition of personal dictionaries so that students create with lots of writing independence. Movement VI indicates immersion into process writing, or the writing process. Also recursive in nature, such a writer's workshop format sees students brainstorming, prewriting, drafting, editing, conferencing, revising, rewriting, and publishing.

Writing is an essential vehicle for literacy development with second-language learners. It allows for high context joined with high challenge. The phonetic connections to be made through key word work should not be ignored. They are natural and coherent complements to all other reading and writing instruction.

NOTES

1. Sylvia Ashton-Warner, *Spearpoint: Teacher in America* (New York: Vintage, 1972), 103.
2. Ashton-Warner, *Spearpoint*, 103.
3. Sylvia Ashton-Warner, *Spinster* (New York: Simon & Schuster, 1959), 190–91.
4. Nina Zaragoza and Eric Dwyer, *Look I Made a Book* (New York: Peter Lang, 2005).
5. Regie Routman, *Writing Essentials: Raising Expectations and Results while Simplifying Teaching* (Portsmouth, NH: Heinemann, 2005).
Vicki Spandel, *Creating Young Writers: Using the Six Traits to Enrich Writing Process in Primary Classrooms. 3rd ed. Creating 6-Trait Revisers and Editors Series* (Upper Saddle River, NJ: Prentice Hall, 2011).
6. Sylvia Ashton-Warner, *Teacher* (New York: Simon & Schuster, 1963), 57.
7. Ashton-Warner, *Spearpoint*, 109.
8. Katie Johnson, *Doing Words* (Ann Arbor: MI: Braun-Brumfield, 1997), 11–12.
9. Erik Erikson is famous for naming the development stages that children traverse through. He names eight stages. The first four are Trust, Autonomy, Initiative, and Industry.
10. Bill Cliett, *Sylvia Ashton-Warner's Key Vocabulary: The Right Way to Teach Your Child* (Amazon Kindle, 2010).

11. Katie Johnson, *More Than words* (Tucson, AZ: Zephyr Press, 1995), 10.

12. These two authors have produced a voluminous corpus of literature. Discussions about the importance of context can be found in *Negotiating Identities: Education for Empowerment in a Diverse Society* by Jim Cummins and *Second Language Acquisition and Second Language Learning* by Stephen Krashen.

13. Lucy Calkins and Abbey Oxenhorn, *Small Moments* (Portsmouth, NH: Heinemann, 2003), iv.

14. Calkins and Oxenhorn, *Small Moments*, 8.

15. Calkins and Oxenhorn, *Small Moments*, 63.

16. Zaragoza and Dwyer, *Look I Made a Book*, 38.

17. Ashton-Warner, *Teacher*, 52.

Chapter 7

The Whimsy of Key Words

Literacy is about making meaning. The task for young children entering the literate world is to make meaning of the symbolic representations that fill their environment. At the same time, there is the challenge to understand the messages that surround their lives, to take in voluminous inputs and sort it all out into meaningful, serviceable knowledge. Literacy is often about dealing with the paradoxes, inconsistencies, and puzzlements that arise from the complex state of being human.

Darlita, who is six years old, has chosen to be at the key word table in her first-grade class. Her teacher welcomes her with a standard key word question—

"What is your word going to be for today?" asks the teacher.

At times, this first question fails to elicit the word that is key for that child, or even any word at all. This time, however, the question does its magic right off.

"Richie," says Darlita. "I want Richie. He's my brother."

The teacher senses the phonemic door opening. "Rrrrrrr—ichie. What is the first sound that you hear?"

Quick on the draw, Darlita affirms, "r," and then she quickly writes the letter on the key word card in front of her.

"Good thinking!" says her teacher. "Only, here's something to remember. When it's somebody's name, what kind of letter do we use for the first letter?"

"I know . . . it's supposed to be a big R . . . but Richie is little. He's my little brother, so the letter needs to be little."

Darlita's teacher suspected that here was a teachable moment, but also couldn't (and didn't want to) escape the whimsical paradox now in the atmosphere.

"I see what you're saying. But there has to be a capital letter. It's also called upper case. So that's a problem. Your key word has to have a first capital letter, but you want it to be little. Hm."

Darlita's wheels were turning. "I can write R, but I can make it really tiny."

That's how Darlita's newest key word became Richie.

On every occasion that Darlita chose to go to the key word table, she read through her quite full key word ring. Smack dab in the middle of the stack of cards was a card that at first appeared to be blank. On closer examination, in the upper-left-hand corner was a word in miniscule handwriting font: Richie.

KEY WORDS AND THE CREATIVE SPIRIT

Doing key words is a creative activity. In its purest form, flushing out the key vocabulary of children in a classroom is meant to release the creative vent. It is no coincidence in the iconic rooms of Sylvia Ashton-Warner and Katie Johnson that the output time of the school day was filled with the materials of creativity, from clay to tempra-like paint. As with many of Ashton-Warner's innovations, such an emphasis on expressive, artistic creativity presages momentous developments in early childhood curriculum by many decades. The image of children's regular and even expected access to all things artistic anticipates the studio concept that is a hallmark of Reggio Emilia schools. Such studios have been given the name *ateliers* and are vital creative spaces in the environment.

In Ashton-Warner's world, here was a studio of artistic creation, but also the playground for play. Contemplating what goes on with key vocabulary work forces the observer to brush up closely to the connection between creativity and play.

When someone says *you're playing with me*, it may be that they are acknowledging being the victim of a practical joke or some kind of intellectual tease or word play. Sylvia Ashton-Warner herself was quite capable of this kind of literary behavior, as she affirmed in no uncertain terms that she was *not* effective as a teacher. In fact, she was not a good teacher at all, so she reported.[1] Furthermore, she disliked teaching. There are passages in her writings where she inches close to attaching the word *hate* to the enterprise of being a schoolteacher. Given that her most famous book, and one of the most widely read books about educating young children, is titled *Teacher*, readers are left to wonder if they are being played.

Ashton-Warner was also adept at telling similar kinds of stories on herself—especially at the hands of children she was working with. Such interplays were most lucid as she described her work with American children at the Aspen school. In addition to having to customize to the reality that dogs and other family pets seemed to supplant family humans as key, she would sometimes become tangled in wannadowanna word games. From *Spearpoint*, here is how it went as Ashton-Warner tried to coax six-year-old Candy into a key word dialogue for the first time. Candy wanted *Beverly* as her first word.

"Is Beverly your mother?" I risk.
"I didn' say she's my mother. How come you keep saying she's my mother?"
"Why do you keep saying that I say Beverly is your mother when I don't?"
"Okay, okay, you don't. But she isn my mother, right?"
"I've got it. Beverly isn't your mother."
"You catch on, huh?"
"Catch on what?"
Thrusts forward her small face to mine, her blue eyes blazing. "Don't you unnerstan *anything*?"
"Depends what country I'm in."
"A-huh."
"So Beverly's not your mother. She must be a friend of yours."
Flinging her hands in despair. "She's not my friend, she's not!
"Is she your enemy then?"
"She's not my enemy," resigned. "Right?"
"Wrong."
Pause. Her little white teeth grip together. "Can you *hear*?"
"Can you explain?"
"Beverly's my doll."
"Well why didn't you . . . never mind." Hold up the card. "What's this word?"
"Don't you know *yet*?" and storms off to the clay room to make wild shapes.
Live and survive . . . right?[2]

Interplay is shown to be a crucial aspect of play, which in its own right is shown to be a vital part of creativity. Interplay can be like a dance between contestants who are taking the measure of each other. Teachers are experts in calibrating this repartee so that students gain enough trust to reveal their true selves while at the same time are mindful of social norms, limits, and levels of respect required of children. All of these elements go into the unique culture of a classroom. Classrooms are made up of all the mega-cultures that are enrolled from the community, but at the same time, these microcommunities evolve into cultures of their own.

Regie Routman is a well-known teacher and author who has gained fame as a mentor about literacy. In her book *Writing Essentials*,[3] she tells the story of an elementary class's dissatisfaction with the meager half hour allotted for a writing prompt that was a core feature of a high-stakes assessment being administered in the school. These students were of a unified mind that this amount of time contradicted all they had learned about what it takes to produce good writing.

These students had the poise and whimsy to realize they had come upon the perfect moment to produce persuasive writing in the real world. They could do something that would yield a much better picture of themselves as writers. The whimsy bled into something of an action project. They composed a letter signed "Concerned 4th grade students," arguing for much longer than thirty minutes to "brainstorm, write, revise, edit, and check over our writing." They mailed the letter to their state's department of public instruction. They received a thoughtful and appreciative response.

This state department incident became part of the identity of the class. They went on to write other letters to real-world recipients where they had to be persuasive.

Students sometimes apply whimsy when the school building starts to show its age or structural malaise. Amy Lindahl tells of making do in a dilapidated edifice where one student exclaimed, "There are mushrooms growing out of the ceiling!" But the real whimsy sprouted up as the heating pipes started "clanking with such vigor" that the class decided they had a troll with a hammer living inside the classroom radiator.[4] Many a whimsy story might be the writing products of such unexpected environmental shortcomings.

Many classrooms have class mascots. In and of itself, a mascot is not an indicator of whimsy. The concept of a mascot can become dripping with the cutesy stuff of teacher nostalgia or a presupposition that Disneyworld and kindergarten are practically synonymous, at least with regard to the environment.

However, in *Look, I Made a Book*, Nina Zaragoza tells of a quite whimsical teddy bear named Brownie who was literally elevated to the status of class member. Brownie joined classroom meetings and was in on-class discussions about kindergarten literature. The class speculated about his *Charlotte's Web* opinions and an important question during literature circle was "What would Brownie think?" Brownie's name was on the class list, quite important when attendance was taken. Brownie went home to families on a rotating basis and was instrumental in prompting family literacy writing projects.

Key words are fertile ground for just this kind of whimsy. It is a significant reminder that in the high-stakes world of learning to read, the out-of-the-box, fanciful tendencies of young children advance and do not detract from the skill acquisition that is called literacy. Similar to other dimensions of classroom dynamics, the door to whimsy is opened or closed depending on whether or not there is permission at the gate. Or disapproval in its stead.

COLLATERAL BENEFITS

Word play, fanciful play, and creative production are essential catalysts for intellectual development. They all play [*sic*] into the establishment of a culture of whimsy that has other benefits as well. Classroom management, for example, is well served when students experience the unity and community of participating in mini-projects where there is quirkiness afoot, or where mild zaniness has taken hold. These classroom narratives make for a group identity based on a healthy troupe mentality. This kind of banding together has good potential to inspire cooperative, community-oriented behavior, rather than limit testing and rule breaking.

A corollary dimension of core early childhood pedagogy has to do with motivation. Teachers are constantly surveying their Geiger counters to locate motivational systems that keep children focused, invested, and immersed in the learning experiences of days upon days in the classroom. The unique and capricious facets of classroom life provide just this kind of fuel.

Ms. Rodrego's kindergarten is one of those rare classes that keeps a classroom pet. It's a mouse in a cage, fittingly named *Mouse*. This pet was especially adored by a group of the younger members of the class, children who were just getting accustomed to long school days, separation from family, and the rigors of learning one lesson after another. Ms. Rodrego spliced in decompression times sporadically and strategically throughout the day. Several children would exploit these precious minutes for attention and care showered upon Mouse.

Camille was one of these students who doted on Mouse. She was also a tepid key word participant. She had received some words including *Mom*, *necklace*, *Liza*, and, of course, *Mouse*.

Although she was willing enough to join the key word table, she sometimes arrived with what teachers might call an attitude. One day when she was feeling particularly ornery, she did her fair share of whining about wanting to hold her friend Mouse. Having exhausted the standard teacher rebukes, Ms. Rodrego decided to try humor and lightness.

"Mouse is waiting for you to get your work done."
Just then Camille's whimsy light went on. "Is Mouse doing key words also?"
From Ms. Rodrego, "What do you think?"
"It would have to be a really little card."
"I bet you could cut one out."

In short order, Camille had cut a couple of mini square inch cards to be a personal set for the classroom pet. The writing had, of course, to be miniscule as well, and within minutes Mouse had the words *food, straw, toy,* and

Camille. A paper clip was bent into a round circle that became the key ring, the words were threaded on it, and it clipped around one of the cage wires in plain view for everyone to see and for Mouse to practice reading whenever he was in the mood.

Camille's new card for her key ring read *Mouse got a key word* (see figure 7.1)—a phrase she read with a touch of whimsy whenever it was time to read the ring.

Children's propensity for reductionist handwriting is consistent with many general understandings about development. Lording over a miniature world is the drive that propels dollhouses, train sets, and model horses. The Lego Company has certainly learned the profitability of tiny figures. And then there is the matter of mastery. As children gain proficiency in forming letters and drawing by hand such images as hearts and stars, they do not rest for long on the laurels of a learner's dimensions.

Small motor adeptness compels the five- or six-year-old to shrink the production. There is a surreptitiousness about it all, as if tiny things are confidential, seen only by those endowed with the power. Vying for power is often the modus operandi of so much young child behavior. Being able to find, read, and create things in the world of the tinies is powerful indeed. So is the facility to find hidden items camouflaged out in the world, or better yet to become the camouflager.

This treasure hunt motif may harken back to the Waldo phenomenon that enraptured children when such books appeared some thirty years ago. Hiding and finding are actions that enthrall children, but key word activity is an unexpected place to find such a compunction. Six-year-old Eduardo, a

Figure 7.1 A whimsical key word card

Figure 7.2 "100 tattoos"

member of Ms. Luong's K/1 class, enjoyed Waldo books and perhaps was influenced by them as his class celebrated the 100th day of school. Collections of all kinds cluttered the room as students brought in boxes and bags of items counted out to the exact sum of 100, but no one anticipated 100 to pop up during key word intake time. Eduardo made sure this century mark homage seeped into key word activity because his request for the day was *100 tattoos*. This caption was inscribed on his card, figure 7.2, although it was quite difficult to find given it was buried under the doodle sketches of 100 tattoos.

EMERGENT CURRICULUM

One of the critical decision points that teachers of young children face is how thematic, topical, and project content will take hold inside the classroom. Many process- and dynamic-oriented teachers self-identify as *emergent teachers*,[5] following students' lead and interests. Such an approach is consistent with the general philosophy of child-centered curriculum, which undergirds most contemporary childhood education. Developmentally Appropriate Practice (DAP) is constructed around the consensus viewpoint that teaching uncovers what children know and are interested in rather than covering a preset regimen of content. NAEYC's manual about DAP states that "teachers plan curriculum experiences to draw on children's own interests and introduce children to things likely to interest them."[6]

Of constant dialogue, colloquia, and even debate is the question of how teachers discover students' interests and passions. How does a teacher know what a class, as a group of children, is commonly interested in? Assertive children undoubtedly wear their interests with vociferous expression, but reading every child is not always easy. Of course, there are tried and true topics, usually drawn from science or social studies concepts. But year to year, groups of students land upon investigative interests that rise above others and are not mapped out by prefabricated curriculums. Sometimes such subjects become identified because a key word card has inserted the idea into the class discourse. That is what happened with Eduardo's 100 tattoos. It became a ritual part of the class culture to find the camouflaged word and count up the tattoo drawings. Creative teachers seize hold of such whimsical activity and are able to incorporate prime learning standards into an integrated project approach study so that cognitive and skill rigor is assured, while maintaining a high level of interest among students.

The whole realm of hidden and camouflaged items, unearthing of clues and cues, searching, concealing and discovering, mystery, and solution is rich in integrative potential as well as interest dependability. For example, teachers know that hidden word worksheets are blessings as entry task assignments. Math teachers count on hidden picture graphing puzzles to provide practice in finding X and Y coordinates. It is not a surprise therefore that Eduardo hit upon the disguising aspect of drawing 100 tattoos to make his key word card interactively entertaining.

The *I Spy* series of children's books[7] joins the *Waldo* series as concept books that take on the search and find theme, to an even further degree. These popular picture books can serve as templates for literacy projects pursued by cooperative groups of students or by individuals. When teachers provide empty booklets of any kind, there is a perfect opportunity for giving students the canvas upon which to design and write their own hidden version series. There is always the option simply to staple booklets together with blank writing paper. There are, however, so many other templates for making books to be written and created by students. Two favorite examples are provided in Chapter 8 following a discussion of bookmaking and its link to key vocabulary.

As with the other examples mentioned above, the original impetus for pursuing this emergent theme was one creative key word card that went out of the box from what everyone else was doing. In fact, it was in Eduardo's case a conjoining of two thematic concepts: the allure of conceptualizing unusual collections of 100 together with the fascination to hide, obscure, and conceal.

It is little wonder, then, that in this very same classroom, the key word *magic* showed up on six-year-old Tanya's key word card quickly hole-punched onto her ring. While Tanya continued to love to receive new Movement I key words, she had for some time been producing booklets and pages as a Movement III and IV writer. While Spanish was her home language, Tanya had become quite adept at putting into written English form her imaginative Movement IV thoughts especially when it came to magic. On the first page of her *Magic* booklet, she had written,

> *Samwon* (a friend in her class) *ses a wish ed the wish coms shrt. That's magic.* (Someone says a wish and the wish comes true. That's magic).

Page 2 of Tanya's epic reads *I like to make a br disibir* (I like to make a bear disappear). This statement is followed by the magic words *abracdadra*. Figure 7.3 shows the beginning of an illustrated story bound to hold the reader's interest.

The topic of magic is incredibly rich for building emergent curriculum that is attentive and sensitive to the directions students want to take, while at the same time cognizant of learning targets at a kindergarten or first-grade level. The enormously successful *Magic School Bus* series exploits the scientific thread of magic. As marvels of change, science and the experiments that inhabit early childhood science books hang on the wonder of surprising and magical events when matter is put through any number of investigations. To come full circle, the potential for vocabulary extension and introduction is quite breathtaking when magic, science, and whimsy swirl around in the creative vent.

Figure 7.3 "Once upon a time a boy was going to eat a rabbit and he growled a lot. The rabbit disappeared. The mouse ate the rabbit. Then my backpack."

LIVING AND LEARNING

It can be seen that often these moments of whimsy arise out of the everyday living that is the community of the classroom. The essence of key vocabulary and organic reading and writing rests in the notion that early childhood classrooms are locations of living merged with learning. They symbiotically synthesize into development, growth, and education. Classrooms must be places of true, genuine, and gritty life; it is not a simulation. Near the end of her biography, Sylvia Ashton-Warner surmised about school: "If school is not a place for living, then children get no living."

One translation of *living* and alive environment comes about because the affective, emotional world of children is wholeheartedly welcomed and even venerated. Laughter and tears, joy and anger are natural, normalized feelings and expressions that burst forth regularly and with acceptance. A glance at the classroom schedule codified by Sylvia Ashton-Warner in *Teacher* paints a picture of this emotionally vibrant community better than any socioemotional development treatise possibly could.

She called it *The Daily Rhythm*, which is mapped out in an oscillating pattern of *breathing out*, an extended first period of hands on use of expressive, art, and creative material for unleashing the bubbling and exuberant life each child brings to school every morning, and *breathing in*, an hour during which key vocabulary is generated, organic reading occurs, and lessons are taught. This top of the morning breathing out block of time is accentuated by the following descriptors that are inscribed as actual events listed on the schedule:

- Conversation
- Crying
- Painting
- Quarrelling
- Singing
- Daydreaming

This is a classroom schedule that stands in stark contrast to what is taped to the whiteboard of most current classrooms. It is the picture of a classroom alive with feeling. Such a classroom intones every stop on the volume dial. Ashton-Warner concluded, "If you don't like noise, don't be a teacher."[8]

But then there are times when the only noise in a classroom is pencils scraping and furtive whispers getting hushed between classmates. Every person who has been a school child and anyone who has put in some time as a teacher holds on to a memory about a day in class when a beloved teacher was suffering from laryngitis and greeted her class with a whisper. Even rambunctious groups of young children settle in for a day of silent learning with the most hushed of conversations and exchanges of information. Such a day was what six-year-old Rosa encountered when Mrs. Luong gathered morning circle to tell her class she had lost her voice, her throat felt hoarse, and everyone would be special helpers for the day.

Rosa was out-front in being especially mindful, and in helping the whole class remember that it was a whispering day. The class schedule was followed as usual. And doing key words was most certainly an option as it always was. Rosa joined the key word table. She had a definite idea about what word she wanted for the day: *Shshshshshsh*.

In whispering voice, Mrs. Luong sounded out the *sh* digraph for her sympathizing student who whimsically was adding to her key ring collection this expression for quieting the class down. When the room got a bit loud, Rosa merely flashed her card in full view. This key word moment also became the hub of a phonics lesson later in the week when Mrs. Luong, again at full voice strength, gave an introduction to the sh sound and had the class generate a newsprint list of words including Rosa's friend *Shantelle*, as well as *shout, shirt*, and *sea shell*. Key vocabulary and whimsy had joined forces for another teachable moment.

The key word experience grows out of a creative and even fantastical classroom. Essentially lively classrooms give permission for key words to emerge. Elizabeth Jones in the book *The Lively Classroom* explains that "day to day, the fact remains that actively learning children are often lively and noisy—characteristics routinely suppressed in many classrooms."[9] It is no coincidence that Ashton-Warner's classrooms contained the constant presence of dancing, music, and singing. According to Ashton-Warner's alter-ego character in the novel *Spinster*, "Crying and singing have the same essential quality."[10] All of these forms of the *100 languages of children*[11] fit into contemporary definitions of literacy that honor the multiple ways that learners represent knowledge and express their inner worlds.

A WORKSHOP FOR ADULTS

There is a reverence for creativity and artistry that serves as a foundation for key vocabulary to percolate, bubble up, and become established as a core component of classroom life. It is this very bonding of creativity and key vocabulary that casts naturalistic light on how to bring adult learners to an epiphany about the power of key words, as well as what a process might look like for getting such a program started in any classroom.

Having published *Teacher* and *Spinster* and eventually *Spearpoint* (the Americanization of key words), Ashton-Warner became a sought-after authority and sage for promulgating the system of organic reading. The later years of her professional life, as documented in her autobiography *I Passed This Way*, provide a fascinating narrative of a groundbreaking early childhood educator who was recruited into and apparently took naturally to the environment and mores of the academy world.

Once again, Ashton-Warner demonstrated an education presentiment that places her as a pioneer. At any given educational conference or convention, teachers can be found acting out the very learning behaviors they are being encouraged to take to their young charges. Teachers willingly dive into dance movements and percussion rhythm keeping, play math games, and don dress ups to wear. From a key word standpoint, teachers immerse themselves in learning by plunging their hands deep into clay and dough, mud, sand, and water, paint and chalk, carpentry, and unit blocks. By doing, they learn. Though contemporaneously this style is routine and blasé as a model of teacher training, it was revolutionary in its day when Ashton-Warner instructed interns and protégées to roll up their sleeves and get creative.

Although hounded throughout her life by self-doubt and low self-appraisal as a teacher, Sylvia Ashton-Warner took to this teacher development leadership as if the adult classroom were her eternal playground. Her self-confidence was extraordinary given the responsibility to live up to the mystique that grew as her writing and artistry attained international renown. She had unflappable faith in the process of unearthing key words. She intuitively knew that the child experience of treasuring captions that were attached to meaningful referents could be recaptured by grown women and men who gave themselves over to the simulation.

In her autobiography *I Passed This Way*, Ashton-Warner summarized her approach with regard to adult education:

> I had a technique for teaching adults; I required they returned to their childhood, became threes, fours and fives again, and I simply took the normal sequences of the organic programme . . . Down to the floor everybody, up to eighty a go, everyone back to childhood again, and out would come the key vocabulary cards. What I'd discovered in no time was that whereas the young had difficulty initially in becoming children again, giggling self-consciously, the grandmas were marvelous at it, and very funny about it.[12]

Key word and *doing words* practitioners echo each other with regard to the ease with which they institute an organic reading program. Katie Johnson makes note of how "the beautiful thing about Doing Words, from the teacher's point of view, is that you don't have to work. All I do from 8:45 until

10:00 every morning is listen, spell, and chat."[13] Of course, this effortlessness comes about after deep rumination about the biggest educational issues and nothing short of courageous stance taking on the philosophical playing field of schooling, early learning, and emergent literacy.

The purpose of adult training in key word work is to release the magic of encounters with personal captions called words. Additionally, such sessions, in the form of workshops, seminars, or classes, hold the potential to invigorate the creative writing power within anyone willing to follow the story unraveled by being handed by someone else a key word written out boldly on crisp, durable card stock. For some teachers and parents, this personal key word experience will serve as the catapult to ask that first child, for the first time, "What is your word for today?"

It is vital that teachers new to the key word process respect and take into account the mandate that *doing words* happens within a framework of equity, cultural responsiveness, multiculturalism, and antibias. As is the case with other components of curriculum, the equity dimension becomes historically obfuscated unless teachers are deliberate, intentional, and rigorous in mindfulness about cultural context in this as in all forms of learning.

Below is an outline for common procedures that make up a workshop in key vocabulary.

Key Word Workshop Lesson Plan

Objectives

- Participants will simulate the experience of identifying words "lodged deep in the mind."
- In pairs and in small groups, participants will facilitate recording and conversing about key vocabularies.
- Participants will reflect about the feasibility of applying new emergent literacy knowledge to their own teaching environments.

Output

- Environmental set up material: clay, play doh, tempera paint, bendable wire, material scraps, glue, crayons, markers, paper, cardboard.
- Participants are invited to spend time freely with the materials. Workshop leader provides a suggested instructional prompt: *Use the materials to express something significant, special, meaningful in your life.* Be as creative as you care to.

- Pair up with a partner. Ease into a conversation about your creative process. Share with each other how the act of creating happened.
- Within the conversations, listen for words (images, people, memories, events) that stand out as special—as *key*.
- With intentionality, make note of deep cultural values embedded in conversations and creative output. For example, a partner might talk about family and the role of family in his or her childhood.
- Participants are prompted to listen deliberately for language diversity cues.

Input

- Partners take turns reflecting to each other potential words that were sparked by the conversations.
- When a partner agrees that a word is key, this word is written boldly and clearly on card stock that has been provided. Two or three words may be added to the ring. Partners proceed to hole-punch and loop their words.

Reflection

- Facilitator brings the whole workshop group together to debrief the experience so far.
- Prompting questions may include:
  - *What is it like to see your word written out by someone else?*
  - *What "inner imagery" feelings were provoked?*
  - *What cultural values did either person identify?*
  - *Were any equity or social justice issues provoked?*

Writing Output

- Partner pairs are invited to return to their workplaces.
- Booklets in various forms are provided. Pencils, markers, and crayons are readily available.
- A writing prompt is given: *As I study my key word, there is a story I want to write about.*

Final Debrief

- Volunteers are invited to read aloud from their written booklets.

ADULT LEARNING, KEY WORDS, AND THE EQUITY COMPASS

It is the responsibility of key vocabulary proponents to prioritize investigations into equity, culture, anti-racism, and antibias as information is shared within professional development formats. Unless intentionally adopting a critical lens, adult educators may well become prone to approaching their work within a context of dominant culture paradigms and white privilege. Deep culture informs every form of discourse but such values and perspectives may not be recognized in the middle of a workshop as bearing cultural content. What might follow then is a neglect of social justice and a disregard for highlighting cultural relevance as integral to this inner imagery exercise.

Facilitators of key word workshops are in a position to model the centralizing of equity in the big picture of this literacy topic. Such modeling is meant to infiltrate into professional development sessions as a rule and of all sorts.

Key word work is cultural by definition and its conception (as seen in Chapter 2) was driven by cultural conflict. Workshop facilitators have the opportunity to illuminate the history behind key words, not only because it is a fascinating story but also because it uncovers how this system was a reaction to the colonization of indigenous people. Reclaiming precious words (both for children and adults) can be seen as acts of resistance and empowerment.

At the same time, there are rich opportunities to excavate the way culture informs the manifestation of key vocabulary. When attendees connect and proclaim the cultural content of words that come forth in a professional development workshop setting, they are better positioned to validate the cultural identities of children in their classrooms. Distinguishing key word work as a cultural act counters hegemonic tendencies to view this, and any other form of literacy, as neutral and value-free. As one simple and glaring example, key word programs are mostly found in schools serving entitled students. The postulation that it is rare to find children from marginalized communities getting the chance to do key words serves as a provocative reflection question for any staff training, session, or meeting.

Chapter 5 is devoted to cautions and precautions that are required in order to maximize cultural excavations. Similar themes are in place as facilitators and leaders conduct professional development when key vocabulary is the topic. It is essential that adult learners exercise reflective and critical thinking about their own development as anti-racist and social justice educators. In addition to the recommendations that are offered in

Chapter 5, the following are guideposts to keep in mind when working with adults:

- Scaffold stories of resistance and activism. Education is a political business and many educators comport genuine and committed devotion to change agency. Professional development venues may not feel like environments where permission is given for activism and organizing stories to come forth. Workshop leaders can actively model the welcome and the centrality that these histories warrant.
- Give voice to the cultural values and the socioeconomic conditions that envelope words and memories that surface as the events of a workshop unfold. At one presentation, for example, a common theme that emerged was family vacations and summer trips that sparked warm memories. The facilitator took the risk of contrasting this romantic car trip and travel theme with refugee and immigration stories that had a very different tone.
- Allow and applaud manifestations of linguistic diversity. In addition to affirming key words that are produced in other languages, these examples can provoke instructive dialogue about dual-language acquisition and bilingual development.
- Model critical thinking. Without question, a key word seminar will invoke the legacy of Sylvia Ashton-Warner and will touch on this complex artist's theoretical and existential contribution to literacy's big picture. As an international figure, Ashton-Warner's writing called upon her school experiences in so many different settings, from time spent in Maori communities, to India, Israel, the United States, and Canada. Yet she was a flawed person, fixed in an historical moment. Though she claimed much affinity for cultures other than her own, there is a thread of superiority and class hierarchy in her reflections. Some contemporaries found her manner affected, insincere, and supercilious.
- An aspect of leadership is to caution against pedestalizing heroes, and it is more productive rather to evoke the complexities of personality and the structural forces that shape any individual.
- Situate the pedagogy of organic reading in the big picture of literacy. Such dialogue would explore the meaning of cultural relevancy and provoke participants to think critically about achievement and opportunity gaps, the development of higher-order thinking skills, the literature cannon, and methodologies that are earmarked for particular groups of students depending on sociocultural profiles.
- Teach about the concept of *funds of knowledge*. Use the stories, creations, and key words that participants produce to conjecture about funds of knowledge that could be incorporated into the classroom—funds that a teacher

might not know about were students denied the opportunity to bring in the inner imagery that gets inscribed on key word cards.

THE TEACHER AS LISTENER

Early childhood education mirrors other trends in education when different ideas come into or out of vogue. The arts and humanities have been relegated to a back of the burner position during the most recent decades, and that development has left creativity squished into the background, behind other curriculum priorities teachers feel pressure to address. Yet creativity (what Ashton-Warner called the *creative vent*) is at the root of what it means to unleash the captions of personal key vocabulary. Time blocks that are labeled output and intake stand as metaphors for the rhythm of the creative process.

The metamorphosis of STEM into STEAM, where the Arts are re-enfranchised as a primary domain of early childhood education, holds promise that the creative vent will recapture respect and its fair due. It is no small undertaking for teachers to hold faith in the creative drive of children and to *stand back* (as the Daily Five Sisters would say), thus allowing the process of engaging arts material to take hold. Even Ashton-Warner aficionados have made note of how her art curriculum with young children was often teacher-directed and pigeonholed toward specific skill development that she was in charge of. She felt a need to teach art forms, so students would know what to do with materials. It is no small revelation that on the walls of Ashton-Warner classrooms at different Maori schools, there could be found exquisite chalk drawings fashioned not by the children, but by Sylvia herself—the artiste extraordinaire.

The image of Ashton-Warner as a didactic director in children's creative expression stands as one more contradiction about this very complex figure in education. Sydney Clemen's testimonial treatise to Ashton-Warner is entitled *Pay Attention to the Children*[14] meant to convey the essence of what rocketed this revolutionary teacher to the spearpoint of renown. But clearly, even for this most psychologically sensitive of mentors, it was so very much a challenge to listen for the creativity pumping through the hands-on work of children manipulating the materials of sculpting, drawing, and painting. The need for a teacher to feel as though preplanned instruction is happening is strong enough that even today most art lessons in kindergarten and first grade are structured around a skill objective. Perhaps, Ashton-Warner's listening post was not automatically attuned to this form of children's expression.

However, it was in and through language that Ashton-Warner exercised irreproachable reception of what children were producing. The creative vent of children's talk, in both their second, and first, home language, was something to behold. Most teachers quickly become aware of children's innate ability to draw and create pictorial representations. For some teachers, the corollary is equally true—children are natural poets, creators of word images that are personal, raw, and unique. Such innate poetic endowment was underscored in a personal letter written in 1964 to Ashton-Warner by the British poet Charles Brasch:

> If poetry is naming, as Rilke and others have maintained, and if children start life by naming what means most to them, and from that go on to writing about what means most to them, we might have more poets—and fewer delinquents.[15]

In the impressively researched and eloquently rendered biography of Sylvia Ashton-Warner (*Sylvia!*), Lynley Hood uncovered an appreciation of the symbiotic relationship between children's creativity and children's language. It is an analysis that reaches the heights of the profound in ECE pedagogy:

> when it came to the language arts—talking, writing, and reading—it was the children who taught Sylvia. Talking was what they did best. In hearing their morning talks and casual chatter, Sylvia found such a fascinating reflection of her own inner life, that almost without realizing it, she developed a powerful new skill: she learnt to listen.[16]

These themes of creativity, deep expression of personal imagery, chatter as a window into children's worlds, and listening as the expressively difficult but potentially most significant act a teacher can perform; here are values and premises that coincide with modern-day Reggio Emilia philosophy to an almost startling degree. The chords of harmony that intone representation, symbolism, artistic drive, and especially an honoring of the breathtaking competency of young children are difficult to miss.

As if to underscore the compatibility of organic reading's basic tenets and the explosion of literature emulating from Reggio Emilia theorists, the most famous and time-honored text promulgating this approach is entitled *The Hundred Languages of Children*, a phrase that encapsulates a core idea of this child-centered way of working with toddlers, preschoolers, kindergarteners, and primary-age children. It is a recognition of literacy as the constant endeavor of children in innumerable forms—perhaps and euphemistically, up to one hundred.

Key vocabulary is not claimed as a heralded dimension of Reggio Emilia teaching and learning, but the compatibilities are unmistakable. An image of the young child emerging into reading through the written manifestation of her own words is an opaque mirror of a passage straight out of the *Hundred Languages* text:

> Their environment must be set up so as to interface the cognitive realm with the realms of relationship and affectivity. So also there should be a connection between development and learning, between the different symbolic languages, between thought and action, and between individual and interpersonal autonomies.[17]

The Vygotsky-like refinement that Reggio theory superimposes upon pure key vocabulary instruction is edification of the role of the teacher, as well as all other people who make up the child's social sphere, toward the concept of co-construction of knowledge. The teacher is actively engaged in scaffolding a child's learning so that edges are constantly pushed and the learner is provoked into higher and higher orders of thinking. Piegetians might name this process as the nudge toward appropriate disequilibrium, in the service of cognitive and emotional growth.

Key vocabulary and doing words fit comfortably into the frameworks that have come to be known as a Reggio Emilia approach. Fittingly, the emphasis on student-teacher interactions that stretch the learner and push the bounds of the zone of proximal development stands as an elegant rejoinder to dilemmas posed by STEM priority and the uncertain injection of an Arts dimension.

Although the tradition and history of key vocabulary is firmly rooted in creative arts as the fountain from which words gusher up, there is a STEM quality to these processes that is undeniable and enlightening as one roadmap into future permutations of ECE literacy. Although the STEM connection might be drawn from many angles, a most apparent one is to pose the question: where is science in the key words of children?

While computers, television, rocketry, and superheroes most certainly claim their portion of key ring entries, it is the quiet, almost hushed, presence of nature that prompts raised eyebrows in our materialistic and technological epoch in educational history. Paying attention to the children means appreciating how a young child sitting in a kindergarten seat is also a naturalist attuned to the cycles of the outside world. How might a teacher tap into this botanical and zoological curiosity and passion? There are clues among the key words.

Below are lists of key words or key word phrases culled from a sample of key word rings that belong to children in kindergarten and K/1 classrooms. Some of the student authors have been introduced in other chapters.

Table 7.1 Key Words with a Nature Theme

praying mantis egg
shark
whale
hamster
bird
flowers
cats and dog
monkey
spider web
dog-tail butterfly
mouse
turtle
baby spider
squirrel
dinosaur
tigre
pinecone
apple
owl
rainbow
butterfly
dog
bunny
spring
garden
walking stick
leaf bug
newt
grass hopper
caballo
rabbit
pumpkin

Several of these words ring familiar as the stuff of childhood. Certainly, authors of children's books are quick to fabricate families of monkeys, frogs, hippos, and horses for all kinds of fantastical tales. However, the lists above also convey the message that children bring funds of knowledge into the classroom.

Even within the confines of an indoor environment, inside of an urban school, placed within the setting of a busy and bustling city, children's minds, when asked what their word is today, often wander off to idyllic natural scenes. It is the nature within the native imagery. Figure 7.4 shows a collection of many of these words, as generated by a variety of different students.

The Whimsy of Key Words 127

Figure 7.4 Nature words on the rings

NATURE WORDS ON THE RINGS

Nature and creativity merge in the key vocabulary story because both concepts are grounded in beauty. For example, even while the Aspen phase of the Sylvia Ashton-Warner story was marked by upheaval and turmoil, the backdrop of the "unreal beauty of the valley in autumn" constantly countervailed the events taking place. The majesty of nature is an important leitmotif for taking in and understanding the full breadth of the key vocabulary story.

Anyone of the images conjured up by the nature theme lists above might well be a jump starter for a unit. ECE educators are fluent in topic studies about insects, sea animals, and dinosaurs. The Reggio approach, however, is embedded not in the piling on of information dossiers, but rather in co-construction of knowledge. The role of the curriculum planner in this case is to delve into the elements of any one of these concepts in search of key areas of interest, focusing questions, group or class recruitment of curiosity, and depth and constancy of passion.

Given that a number of the nature items in the lists practice one form or another of camouflaging, once again this theme has so much capital for its scientific, artistic, creative, and unquestionably whimsical potential. Magic, mystery, cycles, and change—they are all books within words, remindful of Ashton-Warner's characterization of Helen Keller's epiphany about water.

Naturalistic intelligence is the most recent invitee to the world of multiple ways that people are smart. It is an intelligence along with all of the others that inspires captions. It is an intelligence that draws together the science, the art, the creativity, and the act of reading the word.

CONCLUSION

Implementing a key vocabulary program entails delving into the inner and individualized worlds of children. While such a program most definitely touches serious and sometimes tender topics about all that crops up in a child's life, there is also revealed much that is quirky, imaginative, and whimsical. Key vocabularies assist teachers in constructing classroom cultures that are unique and are reflective of quaint events, characters, and stories that emerge unexpectedly as the classroom community works together and learns about who they are as a collective group.

When children experience tacit permission to follow whimsical ideas where they might go, the window is open for creativity to soar. The historical roots of the key vocabulary system are grounded in creative process. Children are afforded ample time and materials for output production, and through the use of clay, paint, sand, maché, and all else that makes up an ECE environment, creative expression is unleashed.

The very same output/intake cycle provides the structure for trainings and professional development meant to introduce pre- and in-service teachers to methods of key vocabulary. Based on the concept of confluent learning,[18] participants are given the chance to participate in the activities they may in the future bring to their young students. The power of generating these captions will be observed directly, and such workshops or classes can serve to inspire teachers to institute a doing words program.

Adult seminars and trainings provoke perspectives about diversity and social justice that mirror similar issues raised in Chapter 5. If key word work fails to consider culture, equity, anti-racism, and antibias, it merely becomes one other form of curriculum that sustains and extends dominant hegemony. Facilitators of adult training are vested with the responsibility to ensure that equity is given a central and normalized place in the full process. Care should be taken to check whether class attention to differences, fairness, identity, and equity is getting paid on a regular basis. If not, serious reflection and analysis are called for.

Organic reading and the key vocabulary system call upon teachers to listen with sublime acuity to the expressions of children. Such listening is the pipeline to recognizing the creativity innate in every child. The preeminence of listening stands as a pedagogical philosophy quite akin to the progressive approach that comes out of the Reggio Emilia experience. The Reggio system perceives and expects the educator to be an active co-constructor of knowledge.

Teachers and children co-construct in many languages. The idiom *hundred languages of children* serves as a constant reminder that the interplay of co-construction takes many forms. Classroom culture can inspire unexpected and unconventional turns—moments in the day that deserve the designation of whimsy. Without question, opportunities for whimsy surface as children are immersed in the key word process. Themes that are intriguing to children may well emerge including the magical, the fantastical, and the naturalistic, all of which can be straightforwardly aligned with contemporary emphasis on STEM curriculum. Scientific investigations into the natural world bring out the magic of key words, child-centered curriculum, and the curious, creative mind.

NOTES

1. These kind of pronouncements crop up in several of Sylvia Ashton-Warner's books, especially in her memoir *I Passed This Way*.

2. Sylvia Ashton-Warner, *Spearpoint* (New York: Vintage, 1973), 59.

3. Regie Routman, *Writing Essentials* (Portsmouth, NH: Heinemann, 2005).

4. Amy Lindahl, "When They Tried to Steal Our Classrooms." *Rethinking Schools* 31, no. 1 (2016): 12–17.

5. Luvy Vancgas-Grimaud, "The Command Center Project: Resolving My Tensions with Emergent Curriculum." *Young Children* 72, no. 3 (July 2017): 60–68. Elizabeth Jones and John Nimmo, *Emergent Curriculum* (Washington, DC: National Association for the Education of Young Children, 1994).

6. Carol Bredekamp, *Developmentally Appropriate Practice in Early Childhood Programs Serving Children from Birth through Age 8* (Washington, DC: National Association for the Education of Young Children, 2009), 21.

7. Jean Marzollo and Walter Wick, *I Spy* (New York: Scholastic, 1992).

8. Sylvia Ashton-Warner, *I Passed This Way* (New York: Knopf, 1979), 104.

9. Elizabeth Jones, Kay Stritzel Rencken, and Kathleen Evans. *The Lively Kindergarten: Emergent Curriculum in Action* (Washington, DC: National Association for the Education of Young Children, 2001), 8.

10. Sylvia Ashton-Warner, *Spinster* (London: Secker & Warburg, 1958), 51.

11. Carolyn P. Edwards, Lella Gandini, and George E. Forman. *The Hundred Languages of Children: The Reggio Emilia Approach* (Greenwich, CT: Ablex, 1994).

12. Ashton-Warner, *I Passed This Way*, 441.

13. Katie Johnson, *Doing words* (Ann Arbor, MI: Braun-Brumfield, 1997), 11.

14. Sydney Gurewitz Clemens, *Pay Attention to the Children: Lessons for Teachers and Parents from Sylvia Ashton-Warner* (Napa, CA: Rattle OK, 1996).

15. Linley Hood, *Sylvia!: A biography of Sylvia Ashton-Warner* (Auckland: Viking, 1989), 177.

16. Hood, *Sylvia!*, 135.

17. Carolyn P. Edwards, Lella Gandini, and George E. Forman. *The Hundred Languages of Children: The Reggio Emilia Approach—Advanced Reflections* (Greenwich, CT: Ablex, 1998), 61.

18. *Confluent learning* is a term suggesting that adult learners come to best understand child learning processes and styles when they engage with the same materials they provide inside classrooms for children.

Chapter 8

Books

Authored and Produced in the Classroom

What is a teacher to do when she does not have at hand the reading resources needed in order to teach reading with all cylinders firing? Suppose the most research-evidenced and perspicacious thinking about emergent literacy was available to ponder about, but there was a dearth of actual material that could be put into children's hands. What if a teacher had been given literally nothing but a chalk board and the command to "bring them to grade level?"

This seemingly far-fetched scenario is pretty much the condition presented to Sylvia Ashton-Warner as she took up a new classroom in 1945 in a town named Waiomatatini on the coast of New Zealand. It is the condition that motivated her to continue the teaching practice that became emblematic of her continual drive to merge the artist within herself together with her persona as a teacher. She created reading basals that, minus her artistic zeal, would never have seen the light of day, or more to the point, would never have been taken in by the eyes of emergently literate Maori children.

The following is an extended excerpt from Ashton-Warner's autobiography, *I Passed This Way*. It is quoted extensively here because it is Ashton-Warner's writing at its best and reflects better than anything else could how she arrived at being a producer of basals written from an appreciation of the need for individualized differentiation—a pedagogical revelation that predates the infusion of differentiation into common curricular vernacular by about sixty years.

> The department of Maori education kept the Maori infant rooms faithfully supplied with stacks of those alien reading books which had originated in

America, Janet and John . . . It's an arduous undertaking trying to turn one race into another, involving both force and failure, so for little other reason than to make teaching easier I plunged in and made hundreds of Maori infant reading books.

(T)here was no duplicating machine or Xerox; all by my own hand. But those only came to thirty-two whereas my roll swung from forty-five to near seventy. So I made dozens and dozens more, every week, to accompany the weekly themes. Songs and verses so far for the Maori infant room—about 1945 to 1949—were still English, all about squirrels and their nut problems, red robins in the snow—I didn't see a robin till 1970 in Colorado—and skinny little English boys in long trousers—shorts are worn in this country from small boys to big men . . . and about falling leaves, whereas all New Zealand trees are evergreen.[1]

The need for cultural relevancy in the books designed for learning to read was thus insightfully argued.

Ashton-Warner went on to describe how she took large rolls of brown paper and made "huge" books to lay on the ground so that groups of children could read them all at the same time. Today, this would be called a guided reading lesson and the books would be called *big books* that adorn most early childhood education classrooms. They are a staple.

Hundreds of books. Here is an image that is more than daunting. It turns out that Ashton-Warner repeated the same kind of enterprise when she was working with American children some twenty-five years later. "Spare us from Dick and Jane" were the exact words she groaned in her account of teaching in America, *Spearpoint*, and thus she went about creating easy readers for the children she was working with at the Aspen Community School. Her guiding principle was to write books derived from children's own key vocabulary—"from their own lives." A theme that threaded through many of them was about Daddy going away—to work, or "Daddy going away for good."[2]

The infant reading books that Ashton-Warner wrote and illustrated, though simple and word-concise, expressed an emotional inner life hard to find in today's reading instruction publishing catalogue. Perhaps, there is poetic justice in a historical truth that is almost too bemoaning to bear. Ashton-Warner met only frustration in her attempts to get these gems published. Interest was shown, but actual publication never came to fruition. She became convinced that a set she had entrusted to a New Zealand publisher was burned or came to some other nefarious end.

Not even one example of these treasures has survived the drama of Ashton-Warner's publishing travails—either the Maori collection of hundreds or the sets she reported about from Colorado. These tales of publishing frustration are documented in her autobiography and in her biographer's extensive research. In fact, Lynley Hood summed up her own frustrated pursuit in a personal communication:

> So sorry, I had no luck in my search for Sylvia's infant readers. I looked in all the archives that had any of her material, and in any existing files of the period at schools where she taught—and I asked everyone who recalled seeing the readers. Some readers may have survived in a box of forgotten papers somewhere, but if Sylvia didn't sign the pictures they would probably not be recognized as her work.
> That's the frustrating reality.[3]

What is left therefore for today's educator are the stories alluded to above and a proposition: if a child is given an easy (breakthrough) reader book using one or several of her key words, written expressively for her eyes, the potential benefits are profound:

- There will be an emotional connection to the story, even if written in the simplest of form.
- The child sees one of her key words lifted from a key word card and transferred to a book form.
- Function words such as *the, and,* and *then* are used in the context of a book written especially for the child.
- The practice of differentiation is taken to a new and different level. It is differentiation of content.
- The teacher demonstrates herself to be a creative writer and artist. She is modeling what she teaches.
- A collateral benefit is the display of caring and valuing that is expressed when a teacher communicates to a child "I care about you enough to write a story about something in your life."

The process of bookmaking infuses into classrooms a fluidity with regard to literature and stands as a celebration of the creative vent. In most of her seminal texts about reading and writing, Regie Routman centralizes teacher- and student-produced books as essential members of the classroom library.[4] One especially revealing story she tells is of an elementary student who struggled in reading but was a brilliant artist. She collaborated with this child to produce "a beautifully illustrated" book about space that he would read to anyone who would listen.

Siri Christensen gained fame in the Federal Way, Washington School District, because not only did she teach poetry to young children, she wrote many of the poems herself. She used a standard format of the time:

newsprint charts that hung from display easels so that students could utilize a pointer to track each word. But then, each child (and family) received a bound copy of her set of poems. The teacher can show herself to be a writer. And to be a poet.

Without question, Sylvia Ashton-Warner set a herculean standard as the creator of hundreds of books iconographed for individual children. That they have disappeared adds to the mystique that characterizes this teacher's profile. Teachers in today's classrooms are not going to write hundreds of books, a new set every year for a new group of students. However, if only just one per child, today's twenty-first-century teacher blazes a best differentiation practice when undertaking the venture of creating such singular basals. The product might be a collaboration between student and teacher or might be solely teacher-crafted. But the seeds that germinate these gems are invariable: the key word rings that hang on hooks or are housed in shoe boxes, each a glossary tied to every individual child.

The term *classroom publishing* immediately connotes student-created material and, as the examples above demonstrate, there is potential for this concept to extend to teacher-produced artifacts as well. The unifying element is that the classroom library (hopefully outfitted with the best, most diverse, and exceedingly culturally relevant children's literature) is also filled with the cultural artifacts of the very community that populates the room for a full year. In her chronicle about literacy in a kindergarten classroom, a book entitled *Look, I Made a Book*, Nina Zaragosa captures an image of anticipation as her year begins.

> We have at least 100 empty book covers done and already the room is surrounded with literacy . . . I expect these children to read in no time. I can't wait![5]

There are dozens and dozens of templates for the creation of empty books, just itching to become filled with student, teacher, or collaborative writing.

Boxes 8.1 and 8.2 offer the designs for two book constructions ready and waiting for authorship, be it five-year-old novice or teacher artiste.

The book design that is depicted in box 8.1 comes by way of author Nina Zaratoga who is quoted above. A child's thrill to have in hand a hardcover book ripe for her own published opus is easy to imagine. Equally straightforward is to visualize how a teacher can utilize this template to write a personalized book gifted to a breakthrough reader ready to be delighted by her key word as subject of a bound volume. The instructions for creating these empty bound books are as follows:

BOX 8.1 MAKING BOOK COVERS

Materials

17-by-12-inch piece of contact paper or regular construction paper
Two 6-by-9-inch pieces of cardboard
Scissors
Glue (a glue stick is easiest and neatest)
Writing paper (8 ½ by 11 inches)

Procedures

1. Place construction/contact paper sticky side up and glue the two pieces of cardboard side by side in the center, leaving approximately ½ inch between the two pieces of cardboard.
2. Cut the corners of the construction paper/contact paper off and fold sides over onto the cardboard (just like wrapping a present).

Paper for inside the cover

1. Put one piece of blank white paper under three sheets of writing paper.
2. Fold papers in half and staple together at the fold.

Putting paper inside cover

1. Put glue on the back cover and adhere last sheet of stapled paper.
2. Adjust papers for opening and closing the book.
3. Add any other personal touches you like (pockets for cards to borrow, binding tape on spine to add more color, and so on).

(Courtesy of Nina Zaragoza, 2005)

Finally, a bookmaking chapter is incomplete without paying homage to the *helicopter and port* template. Below are listed the steps for this assembly. Here is a style of making empty books that requires no stapling.[6] There is something elegant about a classroom book construction that fits a page with a second page, culminating in a "presto" book, ready to be filled with the imagination and inner imagery of the apprentice author.

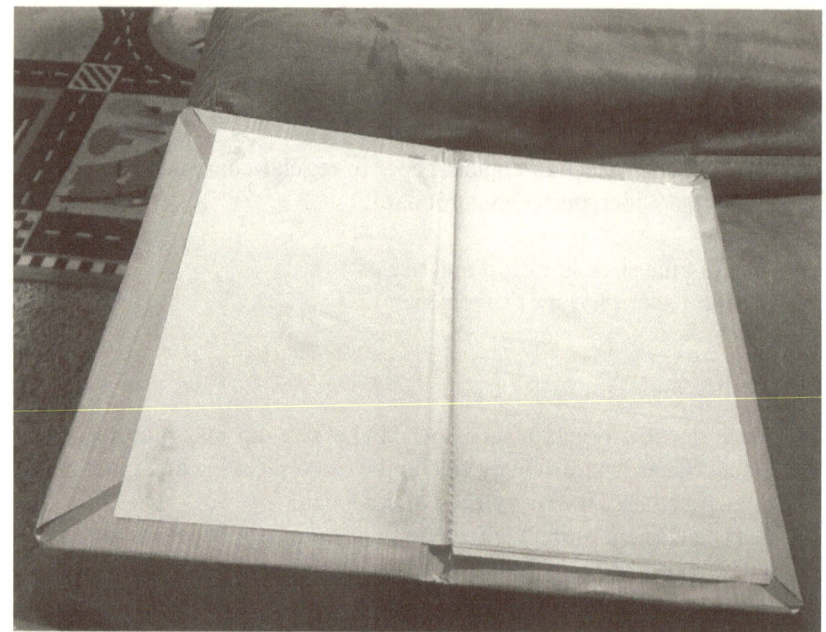

Figure 8.1 Empty book at the ready

Figure 8.2 Bound book cover all set for a student author

> ## BOX 8.2 THE HELICOPTER AND PORT BOOK
>
> **Materials**
>
> Two sheets of standard 8 ½ by 11 copy paper.
> Scissors
>
> **Procedures**
>
> 1. Work with one sheet of paper. Set the other sheet aside.
> 2. Fold sheet # 1 in half lengthwise (hot dog style).
> 3. Measure and dot the middle point, 5 ½, lengthwise at the crease (ballpark measuring is fine).
> 4. Make a 2 ⅛-inch cut starting at the crease from the dot going horizontally. Once unfolded, this will make a slit in the middle of the paper. This sheet is *the port*. Set it aside.
> 5. Work with sheet # 2. Fold it in half widthwise (hamburger style). Open the fold, revealing a crease down the middle.
> 6. Cut two slits along the crease from the top and the bottom. Stop about one-third down for each slit.
> 7. On one half of the paper, curl the sides in order to make a tube. This is *the helicopter*.
> 8. Take hold of the helicopter tube and fly/guide it into the slit of the port.
> 9. Flatten both papers until voila! There is a book.
> 10. The book has four pages.

The procedure is, in a way, organic, and thus is so fitting as the receptacle for the literacy movements that are composed out of the key icons deep in the precious vocabulary of every child.

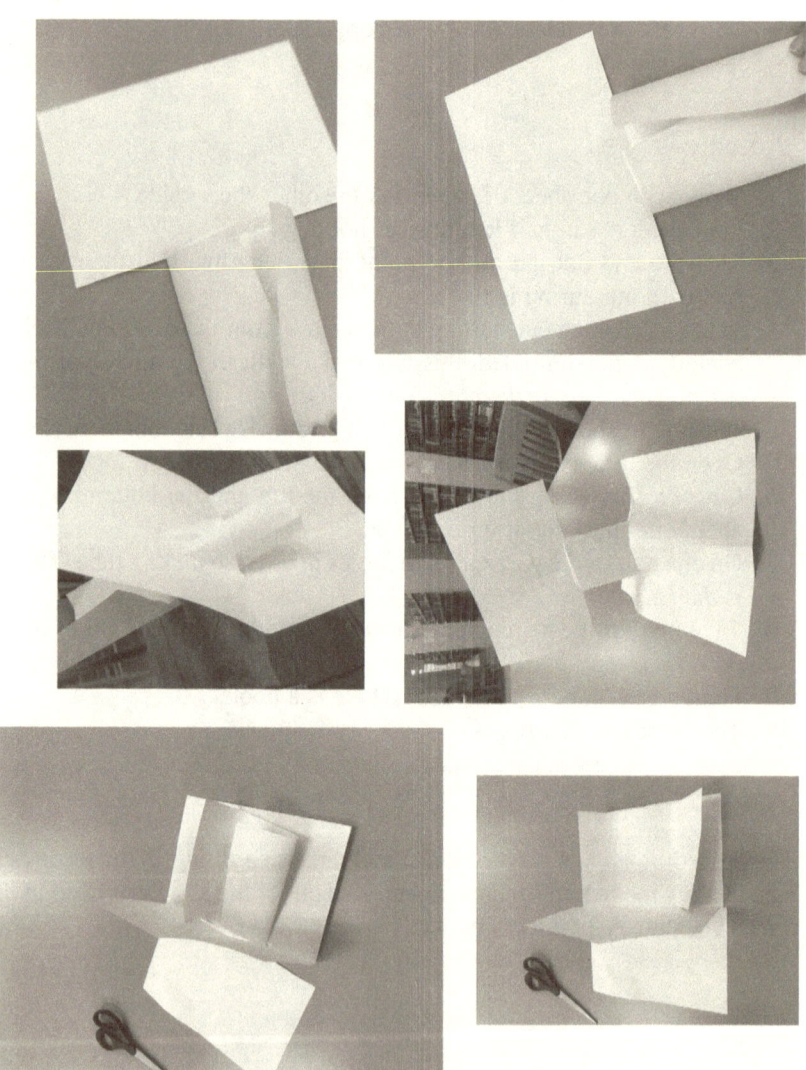

Figure 8.3 Helicopter and port book. Look! No staples

Figure 8.4 Helicopter and port book. Let the writing begin

NOTES

1. Sylvia Ashton-Warner, *I Passed This Way* (New York: Knopf, 1979), 327.
2. Sylvia Ashton-Warner, *Spearpoint: Teacher in America* (New York: Vintage, 1970), 128.
3. Lynley Hood, personal communication.
4. See especially, *Writing Essentials, Reading Essentials, and Invitations*.
5. Nina Zaratoga and Eric Dwyer, *Look, I Made a Book: Literacy in a Kindergarten Classroom* (New York: Peter Lang, 2005), 16.
6. The author is indebted to Linda Wheeler, revered librarian in the Highline, WA, School District, for sharing this design.

Bibliography

Ada, Alma Flor, and Elivia Savadier. *I Love Saturdays y domingos*. New York: Aladdin, 2002.
Ashton-Warner, Sylvia. *I Passed This Way*. New York: Knopf, 1979.
Ashton-Warner, Sylvia. *Spearpoint: Teacher in America*. New York: Vintage, 1972.
Ashton-Warner, Sylvia. *Spinster*. London: Secker and Warburg, 1958.
Ashton-Warner, Sylvia. *Teacher*. New York: Simon & Schuster, 1963.
Bauer, Eurydice Bouchereau, and Beatriz Gurrero, "Young Children's Emerging Identities as Bilingual and Biliterate Students." In *Language, Learning and Culture in Early Childhood: Home, School and Community Contexts*, edited by Jim Anderson, Ann Anderson, Jan Hare, and Marianne McTavish, 19–49. New York: Routledge, 2015.
Bialystock, Ellen. "Reshaping the Mind: The Benefits of Bilingualism." *Canadian Journal of Experimental Psychology* 65, no. 4 (2011): 229–35.
Bouchey, Gail, and Joan Moser. *The CAFE Book: Engaging All Students in Daily Literacy Assessment and Instruction*. Portland, ME: Stenhouse, 2008.
Bouchey, Gail, and Joan Moser. *The Daily 5: Fostering Literacy Independence in the Elementary Grades*, 2nd ed. Portland, ME: Stenhouse, 2014.
Bredekamp, Carol. *Developmentally Appropriate Practice in Early Childhood Programs Serving Children from Birth through Age 8*. Washington, DC: National Association for the Education of Young Children, 2009.
Calkins, Lucy, and Anne Oxenhorn. *Small Moments*. Portsmouth, NH: Heinemann, 2003.
Chatzipanteli, Athanasia, Vasilis Grammatikopoulos, and Athanasios Gregoriadis. "Development and Evaluation of Metacognition in Early Childhood Education." *Early Child Development and Care* 184, no. 8 (2013): 1223–32.
Christie, J. F., Billie Enz, and Carol Vukelich. *Teaching Language and Literacy: Preschool through the Elementary Grades*. Boston, MA: Pearson, 2007.
Christie, J. F., Enz, B. J., and Vukelich. *Teaching Language and Literacy: Preschool through the Elementary Grades*, 3rd ed. New York: Pearson.

Clemens, Sydney Gurewitz. *Pay Attention to the Children: Lessons for Teachers and Parents from Sylvia Ashton-Warner*. Napa, CA: Rattle OK, 1996.

Cliett, Bill Cole. *Sylvia Ashton Warner's Key Vocabulary: The Right Way to Teach Your Child*. Amazon Kindle, 2014.

Conboy, Barbara. "Neuroscience Research: How Experience with One or More Languages Affects the Developing Brain." State Advisory Council on Early Learning and Care: California's Best Practices for Young Dual Language Learners: Research Overview Papers, 1–50, 2013.

Cronin, Sharon, ed. *Soy Bilingue: Adult Dual Language Model*. Seattle, WA: Center for Linguistic and Cultural Democracy, 2008.

Cummins, Jim. *Negotiating Identities: Education for Empowerment in a Diverse Society*. Los Angeles: California Association for Bilingual Education, 2001.

Cunningham, Anne E., Jamie Zibulsky, and Mia D. Callahan. "Starting Small: Building Preschool Teacher Knowledge That Supports Early Literacy Development." *Reading and Writing* 22, no. 4 (April 2009): 487–510.

Derman-Sparks, Louise, and Julie Olsen Edwards. *Anti-Bias Education for Young Children and Ourselves*. Washington, DC: National Association for the Education of Young Children, 2010.

Diller, Debbie. *Literacy Work Stations: Making Centers Work*. Portland, ME: Stenhouse, 2003.

Edwards, Carolyn P., Lella Gandini, and George E. Forman. *The Hundred Languages of Children: The Reggio Emilia Approach—Advanced Reflections*. Greenwich, CT: Ablex, 1998.

Erikson, Erik H. *Childhood and Society*. New York: W.W. Norton & Company, 1993.

Gardner, Howard. *Multiple Intelligences: New Horizons*. New York: Basic Books, 2012.

Giroux, Henry A. *Border Crossings: Cultural Workers and the Politics of Education*. New York: Routledge, 2005.

Gonzales, Norma, Luis C. Moll, and Cathy Amanti. *Funds of Knowledge: Theorizing Practices in Households, Communities, and Classrooms*. Mahwah, NJ: Erlbaum, 2005.

Grisham-Brown, Jennifer, Rena Hallam, and Robyn Brookshire. "Using Authentic Assessment to Evidence Children's Progress toward Early Learning Standards." *Early Childhood Education Journal* 34, no. 1 (2006): 45–51.

Healy, Donald. *Native American Flags*. Norman: University of Oklahoma Press, 2003.

Hendricks, Joanne, and Patricia Weissman. *Total Learning: Developmental Curriculum for the Young Child*. Upper Saddle River, NJ: Pearson, 2006.

Hodges, Tracey S., and Erin M. McTigue. "Renovating Literacy Centers for Middle Grades: Differentiating, Reteaching, and Motivating." *The Clearing House: A Journal of Educational Strategies, Issues and Ideas* 87, no. 4 (2014): 155–60.

Hood, Linley. *Sylvia!: A biography of Sylvia Ashton-Warner*. Auckland: Viking, 1989.

Huerta, Teresa, M., and Carmina M. Brittain. "Effective Practices That Matter for Latino Children." In *Handbook of Latinos and Education: Theory, Research, & Practice*, edited by Enrique G. Murillo, 391–97. New York: Routledge, 2009.

Johnson, Katie. *Doing Words*. Ann Arbor, MI: Braun-Brumfield, 1997.

Johnson, Katie. *More Than Words*. Tucson, AZ: Zephyr Press, 1995.

Jones, Elizabeth, Kay Stritzel Rencken, and Kathleen Evans. *The Lively Kindergarten: Emergent Curriculum in Action*. Washington, DC: National Association for the Education of Young Children, 2001.

Jones, Elizabeth, and John Nimmo. *Emergent Curriculum*. Washington, DC: National Association for the Education of Young Children, 1994.

Krashen, Stephen D. *Second Language Acquisition and Second Language Learning*. London: Pergamon Press, 1981.

Lindahl, Amy. *When They Tried to Steal Our Classrooms*. Rethinking Schools 31, no. 1 (2016): 12–17.

Long, Rachel, and Debora Harris. "Using Literacy Centers to Differentiate Instruction in the Kindergarten Classroom." Annual Conference of the National Association for the Education of Young Children. Dallas, TX: National Association for the Education of Young Children, 2008.

Meeteren, Beth Dykstra Van, and Lawrence T. Escalada. "Science and Literacy Centers." *Science and Children* 47, no. 7 (2010): 74–78. Arlington, VA: National Science Teachers Association.

Montgomery, Winifred. "Creating Culturally Responsive, Inclusive Classrooms." *Teaching Exceptional Children* 33, no. 4 (2001): 4–9.

Morrow, Lesley Mandel. *Literacy Development in the Early Years*. Boston, MA: Pearson, 2009.

National Association for the Education of Young Children. *Using Literacy Centers to Differentiate Instruction in the Kindergarten Classroom*, 2009.

Petersen, Evelyn A. *A Practical Guide to Early Childhood Curriculum: Linking Thematic, Emergent, and Skill-Based Planning to Children's Outcomes*, 2nd ed. Boston, MA: Allyn & Bacon, 2003.

Pinkwater, Daniel. *The Big Orange Splot*. New York: Turtleback Books, 1993.

Routman, Regie. *Invitations: Changing as Teachers and Learners K-12*. Portsmouth, NH: Heinemann, 1991.

Routman, Regie. *Reading Essentials: The Specifics You Need to Teach Reading Well*. Portsmouth, NH: Heinemann. 2003.

Routman, Regie. *Writing Essentials: Raising Expectations and Results While Simplifying Teaching*. Portsmouth, NH: Heinemann, 2005

Sheets, Rosa Hernandez. *Diversity Pedagogy: Examining the Role of Culture in the Teaching-Learning Process*. New York: Pearson, 2005.

Sleeter, Christine E., and Carl A. Grant. *Making Choices for Multicultural Education: Five Approaches to Race, Class, and Gender*. New York: Merrill, 1988.

Soto, Gary. *Too Many Tamales*. New York: G. P. Putnam's Sons, 1993.

Spandel, Vicki. *Creating Young Writers: Using the Six Traits to Enrich Writing Process in Primary Classrooms*. 3rd ed. Creating 6-Trait Revisers and Editors Series. Upper Saddle River, NJ: Prentice Hall, 2011.

Stewig, John W., and Mary Jett-Simpson. *Language Arts in the Early Childhood Classroom*. Belmont, CA: Wadsworth, 1995.

Sullivan, Debra Ren-Etta. *Cultivating the Genius of Black Children: Strategies to Close the Achievement Gap in the Early Years*. St. Paul, MN: Redleaf, 2016.

Valentin, Karen. *What Did Abuela Say?* East Orange, NJ: Marimba Books, 2010.

Van Meeteren, Beth Dykstra, and Lawrence T. Escalada. "Science and Literacy Centers: This Win-Win Combination Enhances Skills in Both Areas." *Science and Children* 47, no. 7 (March 2010): 74–78.

Vanegas-Grimaud, Luvy. "The Command Center Project: Resolving My Tensions with Emergent Curriculum." *Young Children* 72, no. 3 (July 2017): 60–68.

Wasserman, Sydney. "Key Words: Impact on Reading." *Young Children* 33, no. 4 (May 1978): 33–38.

Wiltshire, Monica. *Understanding the HighScope Approach: Early Years Education in Practice.* London: Routledge, 2012.

Zaragoza, Nina, and Eric Dwyer. *Look, I Made a Book: Literacy in a Kindergarten Classroom.* New York: Lang, 2005.

About the Author

Cory Gann is a professor emeritus at Central Washington University. He has worked with hundreds of teacher education candidates preparing to take on their own classrooms from preschool through third grade. His courses have included early pre-K and primary curriculum; parent involvement; early childhood learning; and equity, culture, and antibias. For more than thirty years, he has supervised preservice interns in their beginning trials of practicing skills and critical thinking in contemporary classrooms.

Gann's teaching roots date from years as the North Yard lead teacher at Pacific Oaks Children's School and College. He gained a profound admiration for emergent literacy and learned the power of reflective teaching in daily debriefs with practicum students. Prior to his family's move to the Northwest, he taught kindergarten in Los Angeles Unified School District.

Gann's educational passion has been and continues to be about social justice, equity, anti-racism, and antibias. He was an early member of the Culturally Relevant, Anti-Bias Leadership Group (CRAB) and is currently co-chair of The Praxis Institute for Early Childhood Education. He has joined colleagues on numerous occasions for conference presentations about equitable learning environments, teacher diversity, and antibias education.

Gann is "Papa" to his amazing granddaughter, Harlow, and step-grandchildren, Lily and Henry. Together with them, he can often be found deeply engrossed in dramatic play.

www.ingramcontent.com/pod-product-compliance
Lightning Source LLC
Chambersburg PA
CBHW030140240426
43672CB00005B/208